BEST NEW CHEFS ALL-STAR COOKBOOK

FOOD&WINE

FOOD & WINE
BEST NEW CHEFS ALL-STAR COOKBOOK

EDITOR IN CHIEF **Dana Cowin**
EXECUTIVE EDITOR **Kate Heddings**
EDITOR **Susan Choung**
DESIGNER **Courtney Waddell Eckersley**
FEATURES EDITOR **Michael Endelman**
TEST KITCHEN SENIOR EDITOR **Kay Chun**
SENIOR WINE EDITOR **Megan Krigbaum**
DIRECTOR OF PHOTOGRAPHY **Fredrika Stjärne**
DEPUTY PHOTO EDITOR **Anthony LaSala**
ASSOCIATE PHOTO EDITOR **Sara Parks**
COPY EDITOR **Lisa Leventer**
RESEARCHER **Michelle Loayza**
PRODUCTION MANAGER **Matt Carson**
PRODUCTION ASSOCIATE **Virginia Rubel**

CHEF PROFILES
WRITER **Pamela Kaufman**

FOOD PHOTOGRAPHS
PHOTOGRAPHER **Chris Court**
FOOD STYLIST **Justine Poole**

FOOD & WINE MAGAZINE
SVP/EDITOR IN CHIEF **Dana Cowin**
CREATIVE DIRECTOR **Stephen Scoble**
EXECUTIVE MANAGING EDITOR **Mary Ellen Ward**
EXECUTIVE EDITOR **Pamela Kaufman**
EXECUTIVE FOOD EDITOR **Tina Ujlaki**
DESIGN DIRECTOR **Patricia Sanchez**

ISBN: 978-1-932624-61-8

Published by American Express Publishing Corporation
1120 Avenue of the Americas, New York, New York 10036

Manufactured in the United States of America

AMERICAN EXPRESS PUBLISHING CORPORATION

CHEF PORTRAITS (FRONT COVER, LEFT TO RIGHT)
MICHAEL SYMON PHOTOGRAPHER **Ethan Hill**
GRAHAM ELLIOT PHOTOGRAPHER **Peden + Munk**
ANNE QUATRANO PHOTOGRAPHER **Paul Costello**
ERIC RIPERT, TOM COLICCHIO PHOTOGRAPHER **Jake Chessum**
DAVID CHANG PHOTOGRAPHER **Marcus Nilsson**
THOMAS KELLER, NANCY SILVERTON PHOTOGRAPHER **Peden + Munk**
NOBU MATSUHISA PHOTOGRAPHER **Ethan Hill**
GABRIEL RUCKER PHOTOGRAPHER **Bobby Fisher**
WYLIE DUFRESNE PHOTOGRAPHER **Ethan Hill**

CHEF PORTRAITS (BACK COVER, LEFT TO RIGHT)
STUART BRIOZA, DANIEL PATTERSON PHOTOGRAPHER **Peden + Munk**
DANIEL HUMM PHOTOGRAPHER **Björn Wallander**
LINTON HOPKINS PHOTOGRAPHER **Paul Costello**
ETHAN STOWELL PHOTOGRAPHER **Bobby Fisher**
ANDREW CARMELLINI PHOTOGRAPHER **Michael Turek**
JOSH HABIGER & ERIK ANDERSON PHOTOGRAPHER **Cedric Angeles**
BARBARA LYNCH PHOTOGRAPHER **Ethan Hill**
ROY CHOI PHOTOGRAPHER **Bobby Fisher**
NANCY OAKES PHOTOGRAPHER **Peden + Munk**
MICHAEL CORDÚA PHOTOGRAPHER **Cedric Angeles**
JOHN BESH PHOTOGRAPHER **Paul Costello**
CARLO MIRARCHI PHOTOGRAPHER **Michael Turek**
GRANT ACHATZ PHOTOGRAPHER **Ethan Hill**

BEST NEW CHEFS
ALL-STAR COOKBOOK

The Best 100 Recipes from Winners of FOOD & WINE's Best New Chef Award

FOOD&WINE
BOOKS

American Express Publishing Corporation, New York

2000
ANDREW CARMELLINI *p. 130*

- Soft-Scrambled Eggs with Smoked Sablefish & Trout Roe
- Asparagus Salad with Kaffir-Lime Curry & Peanuts
- Fava Bean Crostini with Prosciutto & Mint
- Pappardelle with White Bolognese

CHEFS

2001
WYLIE DUFRESNE *p. 140*

- Deep-Fried Freeze-Dried Polenta
- Banana Tartar Sauce
- Onion-Clove Compote
- Root Beer–Date Puree

2002
GRANT ACHATZ *p. 150*

- Hot Potato, Cold Potato
- PB&J Canapés
- Sweet Potato, Brown Sugar, Bourbon
- Caramel Popcorn Shooters

2003
STUART BRIOZA *p. 160*

- Sweet Corn Pancakes with Mt. Tam Cheese
- Hot & Sour Yellow-Eyed Pea Soup with Chicken
- Rosemary-Buttermilk Crackers with Chanterelle Spread
- Sausage Fried Farro with Shiitake, Radishes & Scallions

2004
GRAHAM ELLIOT *p. 170*

- Fresh Pea Soup with Ham
- Beet & Arugula Salad with Marinated Burrata
- Chicken with Green Beans in Buttermilk-Tarragon Dressing
- Pork Tenderloin with Fried Okra & Pickled Watermelon

2005
DANIEL HUMM *p. 180*

- Fresh Snow Pea Salad with Pancetta & Pecorino
- Tomato & Garlic Confit Focaccia
- Roasted Peaches with Tomatoes, Almonds & Herbs
- Milk & Honey

2006
DAVID CHANG *p. 190*

- Cold Tofu with Chestnuts in Apple Dashi
- Lentil Miso Soup with Bacon Sabayon
- Hand-Torn Pasta with Pickled Tomatoes & Herbs
- Roast Bass with Kombu Butter, Iceberg Lettuce & Asparagus

2007
GABRIEL RUCKER *p. 200*

- Escarole with Pickled Butternut Squash
- Salmon Poached in Cinnamon Butter with Cedar-Planked Porcini
- Chicken Stew with Shiitake & Lemongrass
- Veal Blanquette

2008
ETHAN STOWELL *p. 210*

- Artichoke & Taggiasca Olive Salad with Parmigiano-Reggiano
- Chickpea Salad with Celery, Golden Raisins & Lemon
- Spaghetti with Garlic, Hot Pepper & Anchovies
- Garlic & Rosemary Roast Pork Loin

2009
LINTON HOPKINS *p. 220*

- Sliced Poached Chicken with Baby Turnips & Mushrooms
- Pan-Roasted Clams with Bacon, Bourbon & Jalapeño
- Skillet Corn & Peppers with Cilantro-Limo Mayo
- Pan-Roasted Grouper with Tomato & Butter Bean Salad

2010
ROY CHOI *p. 230*

- Tomato & Tofu Caprese Salad with Asian Vinaigrette
- Curry-Coconut Clam Chowder, Papi-Style
- Grilled Zucchini with Blueberry-Habanero Salsa
- Double Cheeseburgers, Los Angeles–Style

2011
CARLO MIRARCHI *p. 240*

- Sautéed Puntarelle with Dried Cherries & Pecorino Fiore Sardo
- Warm Radicchio with Vin Cotto & Blu di Bufala
- Squid with Citrus, Chile & Mint
- Sea Urchin Linguine

2012
ERIK ANDERSON & JOSH HABIGER *p. 250*

- Dill Pickle Panzanella
- Red Curry Squash Soup with Bok Choy & Pickled Mushrooms
- Chorizo Oil–Poached Red Snapper with Grilled Corn Salad
- Tea-Brined & Double-Fried Hot Chicken

STARTERS

SALADS

PASTA & GRAINS

FISH & SHELLFISH

RECIPES

Thomas Keller's Salt-Baked Branzino with Zucchini Pistou, page 12

FOREWORD

AT FOOD & WINE, chefs are our heroes. That's why, 25 years ago, we launched our Best New Chef awards, celebrating the most talented up-and-comers in America—the men and women we believe to be the superstars of tomorrow. We're proud to say we've helped some of the country's most important chefs launch their brilliant careers.

For this all-star book commemorating the award's 25th anniversary, we've selected one exceptional Best New Chef from each year—starting with Thomas Keller, arguably American cuisine's most inspiring figure—and shared some of his or her best recipes. The range of dishes is remarkable, from an ultra-elegant, barely cooked salmon with pea-wasabi puree (Eric Ripert) to the juiciest, drippiest six-napkin double cheeseburger (Roy Choi). Page through the book and you'll come away with a sense of how the American dining scene has evolved over the last quarter century to encompass chefs' new fascination with things like molecular gastronomy, foraged foods and humble dishes such as ramen and fried chicken.

It's an honor to be able to share the vision of so many leading chefs. Make their recipes and taste a part of America's culinary history!

Dana Cowin
Editor in Chief
FOOD & WINE

Kate Heddings
Executive Editor
FOOD & WINE Cookbooks

THOMAS KELLER

BEST NEW CHEF '88

Thomas Keller may be America's most inspiring chef, a hero to professional cooks as well as to kids headed for culinary school with *The French Laundry Cookbook* in their bags. At The French Laundry in Napa Valley and Per Se in New York City, he creates hyper-elegant yet playful dishes, as in his Oysters & Pearls: a sabayon of pearl tapioca with caviar and oysters. At Ad Hoc in Napa Valley and his Bouchon Bakeries and Bistros, he approaches rustic food like fried chicken and quiche with the same passion for every possible (and inconceivable) detail.

1974 Gets his first restaurant job at the Palm Beach Yacht Club, which is managed by his mother at the time.

DEFINING MOMENTS

Keller cooks whole fish in a salt crust to keep it moist, then serves it with a chunky zucchini-basil pistou—*Provence's version of pesto. It's a fantastic summer dish, especially with the lemony marinated tomatoes.*

SALT-BAKED BRANZINO WITH ZUCCHINI PISTOU

ACTIVE 1 hr   **TOTAL** 2 hr 30 min   **MAKES** 4 servings

¾   pound cherry tomatoes, preferably heirloom
1   tablespoon minced shallot
½   cup extra-virgin olive oil
4   teaspoons fresh lemon juice
Sea salt and freshly ground pepper
6   large egg whites (about ¾ cup), lightly beaten
7   cups kosher salt (about 2½ pounds), plus more for seasoning
¼   cup ground fennel seeds
2   branzino (about 1¼ pounds each), cleaned
1¼ pounds zucchini
2   garlic cloves, thinly sliced
½   cup basil leaves, plus more for garnish

PAIR WITH Minerally, medium-bodied southern French white: 2012 Domaine Houchart Côtes de Provence

1 Bring a medium saucepan of water to a boil and fill a bowl with ice water. Using a sharp paring knife, score an "X" on the bottoms of the tomatoes and blanch them in the boiling water for 5 seconds; drain immediately and chill in the ice water. Drain again. Peel the tomatoes. In a small bowl, toss the tomatoes with the shallot, 2 tablespoons of the olive oil and 2 teaspoons of the lemon juice and season with sea salt and pepper. Refrigerate.

2 Preheat the oven to 400°. In a large bowl, stir the egg whites with the 7 cups of kosher salt, the ground fennel and ¾ cup of water until the mixture resembles moist sand. Spread a scant ½-inch-thick layer of the salt in an oval baking dish large enough to hold both fish. Pat the salt into a neat oval and place the fish on top, belly to belly. Pack the remaining salt on top of and around the fish. Poke a hole into the crust at the thickest part of the fish, behind the heads. Bake for 25 to 30 minutes, until an instant-read thermometer inserted in the hole registers 135°. Transfer the baking dish to a warm place and let the fish rest for 10 minutes.

3 Meanwhile, quarter the zucchini lengthwise and cut out the seedy parts; discard or save for soup. Cut the zucchini into 2-inch lengths.

4 In a small saucepan, combine the zucchini with the remaining 6 tablespoons of olive oil and the garlic and bring to a simmer over high heat. Add the ½ cup of basil leaves and cook for 1 minute. Transfer the zucchini to a blender. Add the remaining 2 teaspoons of lemon juice and 1 teaspoon of kosher salt and pulse to a chunky puree.

5 Run a serrated knife horizontally around the salt mound and carefully remove the top crust. Transfer the fish to a work surface and fillet them, removing the skin. Transfer to plates. Spoon the zucchini *pistou* around the fish and garnish with the cherry tomatoes. Drizzle some of the tomato marinade on top and garnish with basil leaves. Serve.

▲ **1990** Closes the restaurant Rakel in New York City; two years later, he's fired from Checkers Hotel in L.A.

This porridge is creamy and rich with aged Gouda, trumpet mushrooms and Cognac and topped with an oozy poached egg. Keller toasts the quinoa before simmering it, giving the porridge a deeper flavor.

TOASTED-QUINOA PORRIDGE WITH BLACK TRUMPET MUSHROOMS

TOTAL 40 min   **MAKES** 4 servings

1 stick cold unsalted butter, diced
2 medium shallots, minced
¾ cup quinoa
¾ cup chicken stock or
   low-sodium broth
¾ cup milk
3 ounces aged Gouda cheese
   (preferably raw-milk),
   shredded (1 packed cup)
Kosher salt and freshly ground
   pepper
6 ounces black trumpet
   mushrooms, trimmed and
   minced (see Note)
2 tablespoons Cognac
¼ cup distilled white vinegar
4 large eggs
2 tablespoons snipped chives
Maldon salt, for garnish

PAIR WITH Earthy, bright-berried Beaujolais: 2011 Jean Foillard Côte du Py Morgon

1 In a small saucepan, melt 1 tablespoon of the butter. Add half of the shallots and the quinoa and cook over moderate heat, stirring, until the quinoa is lightly browned and nutty-smelling, about 4 minutes. Add the chicken stock and milk and bring to a boil. Cover and simmer over low heat until the quinoa is tender, about 15 minutes.

2 Add 5 tablespoons of the butter to the quinoa a few pieces at a time, stirring, until creamy. Add the Gouda and stir until melted and completely incorporated. Season the quinoa porridge with kosher salt and pepper and keep warm over very low heat.

3 In a medium skillet, melt the remaining 2 tablespoons of butter. Add the remaining shallots and cook over moderate heat until softened, about 3 minutes. Add the mushrooms, season with kosher salt and pepper and cook over moderate heat until the mushrooms are tender, about 8 minutes. Add the Cognac and cook until evaporated. Cover the skillet and remove from the heat.

4 Meanwhile, bring a large, deep skillet of water to a simmer over moderate heat. Add the vinegar. Crack the eggs one at a time into a small bowl, then carefully slide them into the simmering water. Poach the eggs over moderate heat until the whites are set but the yolks are still slightly runny, about 5 minutes. Using a slotted spoon, carefully lift the poached eggs out of the water and transfer to paper towels; blot dry.

5 Spoon the mushrooms into shallow bowls and top with the quinoa porridge. Top with the eggs and garnish with the chives. Sprinkle with Maldon salt and serve right away.

NOTE Fresh black trumpet mushrooms have a rich flavor and meaty texture. They are available at specialty markets and online at *amazon.com*.

MAKE AHEAD The recipe can be prepared through Step 3 up to 2 hours ahead.

Keller's trick for yielding extra-flavorful meat is seasoning the roast a day in advance: The lamb takes on the aroma of garlic and thyme as well as a subtle heat from piment d'Espelette, a smoky, mildly spicy ground pepper.

SLOW-COOKED LAMB WITH CIPOLLINI, DATES, KALE & ALMONDS

ACTIVE 1 hr   **TOTAL** 6 hr plus overnight marinating   **MAKES** 6 servings

One 2½-pound boneless lamb shoulder roast
2 teaspoons piment d'Espelette (see Note)
4 large garlic cloves— 2 very finely grated, 2 halved
2 tablespoons chopped thyme
Kosher salt
¼ cup plus 2 tablespoons extra-virgin olive oil
1 cup oloroso sherry
18 cipollini onions (1½ pounds), peeled
18 Medjool dates (15 ounces), halved and pitted
1½ pounds kale, preferably Lacinato, stemmed and coarsely chopped
⅓ cup marcona almonds
Thin strips of orange zest, for garnish
Sea salt and freshly ground black pepper

PAIR WITH Concentrated, peppery Rhône red: 2010 Domaine la Garrigue Vacqueyras

1 Set the lamb on a work surface. In a small bowl, combine the piment d'Espelette with the grated garlic, the thyme, 1½ tablespoons of kosher salt and 2 tablespoons of the oil to form a paste; rub the paste all over the lamb. Roll up the lamb and tie with kitchen string at 1-inch intervals; wrap in plastic and refrigerate overnight.

2 Unwrap the lamb and bring it to room temperature. Preheat the oven to 500°. Place the lamb in a large enameled cast-iron casserole and roast for 20 minutes, until browned on the bottom. Turn the lamb over and roast for another 10 minutes. Add the sherry and 1 cup of water and cover. Reduce the oven temperature to 225° and braise the lamb for 2 hours. Add the onions, cover and cook for 1 hour longer.

3 Uncover the casserole and cook for about 30 minutes, until the onions have softened and the lamb is fork-tender. Remove the casserole from the oven and stir in the dates. Let stand at room temperature for 20 minutes. Spoon off as much fat as possible from the juices.

4 In a large skillet, heat the remaining ¼ cup of oil. Add the halved garlic cloves and cook over high heat, stirring, until they are lightly golden, about 1 minute. Add the kale, season with kosher salt and cook, tossing, until just tender, about 4 minutes.

5 Remove the strings from the lamb and carve the meat into thick slices. Transfer the kale to shallow bowls and top with the lamb. Spoon the onions, dates and juices all around. Garnish with the almonds and orange zest, sprinkle with sea salt and pepper and serve right away.

NOTE Piment d'Espelette is available at specialty food shops, spice shops and *piperade.com*.

1999 Publishes *The French Laundry Cookbook*, which goes on to sell more than half a million copies and becomes a seminal book for young aspiring chefs.

Macerating peaches, plums and cherries with vanilla and sugar creates a rich juice that is fabulous spooned over silky pudding. Keller serves the dessert with buttery, crumbly shortbread, a staple at his Bouchon Bakeries.

VANILLA PUDDING WITH MACERATED STONE FRUITS & SHORTBREAD

ACTIVE 1 hr   **TOTAL** 1 hr 45 min plus 3 hr chilling   **MAKES** 6 servings plus leftover cookies

SHORTBREAD COOKIES

- 2¼ cups all-purpose flour (10½ ounces), plus more for dusting
- 1¾ sticks (7 ounces) unsalted butter, softened
- ¼ cup plus 2 tablespoons sugar, plus more for sprinkling
- 1½ teaspoons vanilla paste (see Note)

PUDDING

- 1 cup milk
- 1 cup heavy cream
- 1½ teaspoons vanilla paste
- ¼ cup plus 2 tablespoons sugar
- 4 large egg yolks, at room temperature
- 1½ teaspoons unflavored powdered gelatin softened in 2 tablespoons of cold water
- ¼ cup plus 2 tablespoons crème fraîche

STONE FRUITS

- 1 large peach, pitted and cut into ¾-inch pieces
- 2 large plums, pitted and cut into ¾-inch pieces
- 1 cup pitted cherries, halved
- ½ cup sugar
- 1 tablespoon vanilla paste
- 1 tablespoon fresh lemon juice

Pinch of salt

1 MAKE THE SHORTBREAD COOKIES Preheat the oven to 325° and line a baking sheet with parchment paper. In a standing mixer fitted with the paddle, combine all of the shortbread ingredients and beat at medium speed until the dough just comes together. Pat the dough into a 6-inch square, wrap in plastic and refrigerate for at least 30 minutes.

2 On a lightly floured surface, roll the dough into an 8-inch square, ½ inch thick. Cut the dough into 4 strips, then cut each strip into 5 cookies. Arrange the cookies on the prepared baking sheet and bake until golden, 30 to 35 minutes. Immediately sprinkle the cookies with sugar and let cool.

3 MAKE THE PUDDING In a medium saucepan, combine the milk, cream and vanilla paste and bring to a simmer. In a medium heatproof bowl, whisk the sugar with the egg yolks until smooth. Gradually whisk in the hot milk. Return the mixture to the saucepan and cook over low heat, stirring constantly but gently with a wooden spoon, until thickened slightly, about 5 minutes. Remove from the heat and stir in the softened gelatin until melted. Strain the pudding through a fine sieve into a medium heatproof bowl and let cool, stirring occasionally.

4 In a small bowl, whisk the crème fraîche until firm peaks form, then fold into the pudding. Press a sheet of plastic wrap directly onto the surface of the pudding and refrigerate until chilled, about 3 hours.

5 MEANWHILE, PREPARE THE STONE FRUITS Combine all of the ingredients in the top of a double boiler. In the bottom of the double boiler, bring 2 inches of water to a boil and turn off the heat. Set the fruit over the water, cover and let stand for 30 minutes, stirring occasionally.

6 To serve, spoon the pudding into bowls and top with the fruits and their juices. Arrange the cookies on a platter and serve alongside.

NOTE Vanilla paste is available at specialty food stores and online at *kingarthurflour.com*. You can also substitute seeds scraped from half of a plump vanilla bean for 1½ teaspoons of vanilla paste.

MAKE AHEAD The cookies can be kept at room temperature and the pudding can be refrigerated for up to 3 days.

89

NOBU MATSUHISA

BEST NEW CHEF '89

Nobu Matsuhisa has changed how the world thinks about Japanese food. Rigorously trained in classical sushi-making techniques in Tokyo, he came up with his no-rules style while working in Peru, adding global flavors to raw and cooked dishes in a way that was radically inventive. Already presiding over 26 Nobu and Matsuhisa restaurants with business partners Robert De Niro, Drew Nieporent and Meir Teper, he recently launched the Nobu Hotel in Las Vegas (more locations are in the works). Here, he poses with two glowing sushi-rolling mats, graceful as wings.

1967 Begins a six-year apprenticeship at a sushi restaurant in Tokyo.

Tiradito is a Japanese-style variation on ceviche that Nobu helped popularize when he was cooking in Peru. His minimalist version here requires the freshest scallops you can find.

SEA SCALLOP TIRADITO

TOTAL 10 min   **MAKES** 8 first-course servings

12 large diver scallops
 1 tablespoon vegetable oil
Chile paste, preferably *ají rocoto*
     (a hot red chile; see Note)
24 small cilantro leaves
 1 teaspoon fresh lemon juice
Sea salt

PAIR WITH Ripe, fruity junmai ginjo sake: Fukucho Moon on the Water

1 Cut each scallop in half horizontally. Set a large skillet over high heat for 3 minutes. Add the vegetable oil and heat until smoking. Add the scallop slices and sear for 1 minute.

2 Arrange 3 scallop slices, seared side up, on each plate, overlapping them slightly. Garnish each slice with a dot of chile paste and a cilantro leaf. Sprinkle with the lemon juice and sea salt and serve immediately.

NOTE *Ají rocoto* chile paste is available at some Latin American stores and online at *tienda.com.*

A signature at Nobu restaurants, this sweet-savory fish dish has been cloned by chefs all over the world. Nobu marinates the black cod in a good deal of the sake-miso marinade for two to three days, but the fish is also spectacular if you marinate it only overnight in just enough sake and miso to coat.

BLACK COD WITH MISO

TOTAL 30 min plus overnight marinating   **MAKES** 6 servings

3 tablespoons mirin
3 tablespoons sake
½ cup white miso paste
⅓ cup sugar
Six 6- to 7-ounce skinless black cod
    fillets, about 1½ inches thick
Vegetable oil, for grilling
Pickled ginger, for serving

PAIR WITH Spicy, full-bodied
Gewürztraminer: 2011 Navarro
Vineyards Estate Dry

1 In a small saucepan, bring the mirin and sake to a boil. Whisk in the miso until dissolved. Add the sugar and cook over moderate heat, whisking, just until dissolved. Transfer the marinade to a large baking dish and let cool. Add the fish and turn to coat. Cover and refrigerate overnight.

2 Preheat the oven to 400°. Heat a grill pan and oil it. Scrape the marinade off the fish and grill over high heat until browned, about 2 minutes. Turn the fish over onto a heavy rimmed baking sheet and roast for 10 minutes, until flaky. Transfer the fish to plates and serve with pickled ginger.

MAKE AHEAD The marinade can be refrigerated for up to 1 week.

Nobu makes the ultimate chicken teriyaki. His best-ever version, which is incredibly easy to prepare at home, calls for tender chicken breasts, but boneless chicken thighs would be wonderful too.

CLASSIC CHICKEN TERIYAKI

TOTAL 30 min   **MAKES** 4 servings

1 cup chicken stock or
   low-sodium broth
⅓ cup low-sodium soy sauce
⅓ cup sugar
2 tablespoons mirin
2 tablespoons sake
Four 6-ounce skinless, boneless
   chicken breasts, lightly pounded
Kosher salt and freshly
   ground pepper
2 tablespoons canola oil
2 large Italian frying peppers,
   cut into ½-inch strips
Steamed short-grain rice, for serving

PAIR WITH Juicy, raspberry-rich Grenache: 2012 Bonny Doon Clos de Gilroy

1 In a medium saucepan, combine the chicken stock, soy sauce, sugar, mirin and sake and bring to a boil over high heat, stirring to dissolve the sugar. Reduce the heat to moderate and simmer the teriyaki sauce until syrupy and reduced to ½ cup, about 20 minutes.

2 Meanwhile, season the chicken with salt and pepper. In a large nonstick skillet, heat 1 tablespoon of the canola oil. Add the chicken and cook over moderately high heat, turning once, until browned on both sides and cooked through, 8 to 9 minutes. Transfer the chicken to a plate and let stand for 5 minutes.

3 Wipe out the skillet. Add the remaining 1 tablespoon of canola oil and heat until shimmering. Add the pepper strips and cook over high heat, stirring occasionally, until crisp-tender and lightly charred, about 3 minutes. Transfer the peppers to plates. Slice the chicken breasts crosswise and transfer to the plates. Drizzle the teriyaki sauce over the chicken and serve with rice.

MAKE AHEAD The teriyaki sauce can be refrigerated for up to 1 month.

Nobu is as expert with meat as he is with fish. Early in his career, at his restaurant in Lima, Peru, he was grilling beef and making tangy, mildly spicy red chile (ají panca) sauce and spicier yellow chile (ají amarillo) sauce. He serves both sauces with this seared beef tenderloin.

BEEF TENDERLOIN WITH SPICY LATIN SAUCES

TOTAL 30 min   **MAKES** 4 servings

1½ tablespoons *ají panca* (red chile) paste or red hot sauce (see Note)

2½ tablespoons sake

2 tablespoons unseasoned rice vinegar

1 garlic clove, minced

½ teaspoon ground cumin

¼ teaspoon dried oregano

Sea salt and freshly ground pepper

¼ cup grapeseed oil, plus more for cooking

1 tablespoon *ají amarillo* (yellow chile) paste or Scotch bonnet hot sauce (see Note)

1½ teaspoons soy sauce

1½ teaspoons fresh lemon juice

1½ teaspoons fresh yuzu juice or orange juice

2 tablespoons unsalted butter

2 large leeks, white and tender green parts only, cut into ½-inch pieces

4 beef tenderloin steaks, about 1 inch thick

PAIR WITH Aromatic, berry-dense Washington state Merlot: 2010 Waterbrook

1 Preheat the oven to 400°. In a small bowl, whisk the *ají panca* with the sake, vinegar, garlic, cumin and oregano and season with salt and pepper. Add 2 tablespoons of the grapeseed oil.

2 In another small bowl, whisk the *ají amarillo* with the soy sauce, lemon juice, yuzu juice and the remaining 2 tablespoons of grapeseed oil.

3 Melt the butter in a medium skillet. Add the leeks, season with salt and pepper and cook over moderate heat, stirring frequently, until tender, about 8 minutes; keep warm.

4 Heat a cast-iron skillet. Brush the steaks with oil and season generously with salt and pepper. Cook over high heat, turning once, until browned, about 7 minutes. Transfer the skillet to the oven and roast the steaks for about 5 minutes for medium-rare meat.

5 Spoon the leeks onto plates and top with the steaks. Spoon both sauces on either side of the steaks and serve.

NOTE Peruvian *ají panca* and *ají amarillo* pastes are available at many Latin American stores and online at *tienda.com*.

MAKE AHEAD The sauces can be refrigerated for up to 3 days.

NANCY SILVERTON

BEST NEW CHEF '90

By launching La Brea Bakery in Los Angeles in 1989, Nancy Silverton helped turn Americans on to the possibilities of really good bread. In the late '80s, most of us were content with pale, soft, squishy loaves; Silverton, the gifted pastry chef and cofounder (with Mark Peel) of Campanile, helped change that by introducing the tangy, crisp-crusted, all-natural sourdough breads she'd eaten in Europe. Silverton's love of bread and Italian food is obvious at Pizzeria Mozza and Osteria Mozza in L.A., where she rules the mozzarella bar and creates fantastic dishes like the ones featured here.

1974 While a student at Sonoma State University, she volunteers as a cook in the school's cafeteria kitchen.

For this single-serving frittata, Silverton cooks the eggs gently, then tops them with asparagus, prosciutto and crème fraîche. Since the frittata is not warmed in the oven, it's best to have the toppings at room temperature. Also, keep them near the pan so you can work quickly once the eggs are cooked.

STOVETOP ASPARAGUS FRITTATA

TOTAL 30 min   **MAKES** 1 serving

7 thin asparagus spears, cut on the diagonal into 2-inch pieces
1 tablespoon extra-virgin olive oil
Kosher salt
2½ tablespoons unsalted butter
¼ cup minced shallot
3 large eggs, preferably organic
1 ounce thinly sliced prosciutto, torn into pieces
2 tablespoons crème fraîche, at room temperature
Freshly cracked black pepper
1 tablespoon freshly grated Parmigiano-Reggiano cheese

PAIR WITH Zesty, light-bodied Albariño: 2011 Benito Santos

1 Preheat the oven to 400°. On a rimmed baking sheet, toss the asparagus with the olive oil, season with salt and roast for about 10 minutes, stirring occasionally, until tender.

2 Meanwhile, in a small nonstick skillet, melt 1 tablespoon of the butter. Add the shallot and cook over moderate heat, stirring occasionally, until softened, 3 to 4 minutes. Transfer the shallot to a small bowl; wipe out the skillet.

3 In a medium bowl, whisk the eggs with ¼ teaspoon of salt and 2 teaspoons of cold water. In the skillet, melt the remaining 1½ tablespoons of butter over moderately low heat. Pour in the eggs and cook without stirring until the edge of the frittata has set, about 3 minutes.

Using a heatproof rubber spatula, lift up the edge of the frittata and tilt the pan to allow the uncooked eggs to seep underneath. Continue gently cooking the frittata in this way until almost no egg runs when you tilt the pan.

4 Immediately scatter the shallot, prosciutto and asparagus over the frittata and slide it onto a serving plate. Top with the crème fraîche, pepper and grated cheese and serve warm.

Silverton likes to massage thick dressings like this sweet-salty vinaigrette into sturdy greens with her hands to make sure they're evenly coated. The recipe makes more dressing than you'll need for the salad. Any left over is great as a dip for raw fennel, celery, carrots or other vegetables.

RED ENDIVE & FENNEL SALAD WITH ANCHOVY-DATE DRESSING

TOTAL 35 min   **MAKES** 12 servings

4 large, moist Medjool dates
   (3 ounces), pitted and chopped

6 oil-packed anchovy fillets,
   drained and chopped

2 teaspoons finely grated
   lemon zest

2 teaspoons finely grated
   orange zest

1 teaspoon grated garlic

¼ cup red wine vinegar

½ cup extra-virgin olive oil

2 medium fennel bulbs
   (2 pounds)—trimmed, cored
   and very thinly sliced

8 red endives (1½ pounds),
   leaves separated

2 tablespoons fresh lemon juice

Kosher salt and coarsely ground
   black pepper

1½ ounces Parmigiano-Reggiano
   cheese, shaved (about ⅓ cup)

1 In a medium bowl, using a wooden spoon, mash the dates with the anchovies, lemon zest, orange zest and garlic to form a coarse paste. Stir in the vinegar, then whisk in the olive oil.

2 In a very large bowl, toss the fennel and endives. Add 1 tablespoon of the lemon juice and half of the dressing; with your hands, gently massage the dressing into the endive leaves. Season the salad with salt, pepper and more lemon juice to taste.

3 Line a platter with half of the endives and fennel and scatter with half of the cheese. Repeat with the remaining endives, fennel and cheese. Drizzle some of the remaining dressing over the salad, season with pepper and pass the rest of the dressing at the table.

Inspired by the antipasti at Italian-American restaurants, Silverton developed a sophisticated version for her cookbook A Twist of the Wrist. *It features shredded iceberg lettuce, salami and petite mozzarella balls* (bocconcini), *which she loves because each is a perfect little bite.*

ANTIPASTO SALAD WITH SALAMI & GREEN OLIVE– MARINATED BOCCONCINI

TOTAL 30 min   **MAKES** 6 to 8 servings

3 tablespoons jarred green olive tapenade

¼ cup peperoncini—stemmed, seeded and finely chopped

½ cup extra-virgin olive oil

1½ cups *bocconcini* (about 9 ounces)

1 tablespoon plus 1 teaspoon fresh lemon juice

1 tablespoon plus 1 teaspoon red wine vinegar

1 tablespoon plus 1 teaspoon minced garlic

1 teaspoon dried oregano

Salt and freshly ground pepper

1 small head of iceberg lettuce— halved, cored and finely shredded (4 cups)

6 ounces thinly sliced Genoa salami, cut into thin strips (1½ cups)

6 small basil leaves

½ cup pitted green olives, such as Picholine

PAIR WITH Frothy, berry-scented Lambrusco: NV Venturini Baldini Lambrusco dell'Emilia

1 In a medium bowl, mix the green olive tapenade with the chopped peperoncini and ¼ cup of the olive oil. Add the *bocconcini* and toss well.

2 In a small bowl, whisk the lemon juice with the red wine vinegar, garlic and oregano. Whisk in the remaining ¼ cup of olive oil and season the dressing with salt and pepper.

3 In a large bowl, toss the shredded lettuce and salami. Add the marinated *bocconcini* and half of the dressing and toss well. Transfer the antipasto salad to a platter and top with the basil and olives. Drizzle the remaining dressing over the salad and serve.

MAKE AHEAD The recipe can be prepared through Step 2 and refrigerated overnight.

Silverton is renowned for the obsessive attention she pays to her salads. The key to her kale salad is the layering of many ingredients so that there's something delicious in every forkful.

KALE SALAD WITH RICOTTA SALATA, PINE NUTS & ANCHOVIES

TOTAL 30 min   **MAKES** 6 servings

¼ cup pine nuts

1 small shallot, minced

Finely grated zest of 1 lemon

¼ cup fresh lemon juice

1 tablespoon Champagne or white wine vinegar

1 garlic clove, grated

Pinch of crushed red pepper

½ cup extra-virgin olive oil

3 ounces *ricotta salata* cheese, coarsely shredded (¾ cup)

Kosher salt and freshly ground black pepper

1 bunch of kale, preferably Lacinato (6 ounces), stemmed and leaves torn into bite-size pieces (8 cups)

8 marinated *alici* (white anchovies), drained

PAIR WITH Lively, citrusy northern Italian Pinot Grigio: 2012 Tiefenbrunner

1 In a small skillet, toast the pine nuts over moderately low heat, stirring frequently, until light golden, about 10 minutes. Transfer to a small bowl.

2 In a medium bowl, combine the shallot, lemon zest, lemon juice, vinegar, garlic and crushed red pepper. Whisk in the olive oil until emulsified. Stir in ½ cup of the *ricotta salata* and season the dressing with salt and black pepper.

3 In a large bowl, toss the kale with half of the dressing; add more dressing if desired. Transfer half of the kale to a serving platter and top with half of the remaining *ricotta salata*, 4 anchovies and half of the pine nuts. Repeat the layering with the remaining kale, *ricotta salata*, anchovies and pine nuts and serve.

2006 Partners with Mario Batali and Joe Bastianich to open Pizzeria Mozza in L.A.; they open Osteria Mozza one year later.

91

TOM COLICCHIO

BEST NEW CHEF '91

Tom Colicchio has become the food world's conscience, the chef who other chefs trust for his unvarnished opinions. Whether running his New York City–based Craft empire or appearing as head judge on *Top Chef,* Colicchio sincerely wants to teach and promote good cooking. He also leads by example, creating dishes with clean, assertive, streamlined flavors. His debut menu at Craft, which let diners choose their protein, sauce and accompaniments, epitomized his point of view. Colicchio is also inspiring for his work to fight hunger and nourish kids, testifying before Congress in 2010 in support of school-lunch reform and serving as executive producer for the documentary *A Place at the Table.*

Colicchio makes this sweet-tangy relish with red bell peppers, chiles and freshly shucked corn kernels, which remain crisp during pickling. It's a fabulous accompaniment to grilled meats and seafood.

CORN RELISH

TOTAL 1 hr plus 24 hr pickling   **MAKES** about 6 cups

1½ cups white wine vinegar
¼ cup sugar
1 garlic clove, minced
1 tablespoon finely grated peeled fresh ginger
1 tarragon sprig
1 thyme sprig
1 tablespoon peanut or canola oil
1 small onion, diced
3 Fresno chile peppers, minced
1 red bell pepper, diced
Kosher salt
6 ears of corn, shucked, kernels cut off
5 scallions, white parts only, finely chopped
Cayenne pepper (optional)

1 In a small saucepan, combine the vinegar and sugar and bring to a boil. Add the garlic and ginger and simmer over moderate heat until the mixture has reduced by one-third, about 10 minutes. Remove the pan from the heat, add the tarragon and thyme and let steep for 5 minutes.

2 Meanwhile, in a large saucepan, heat the oil until shimmering. Add the onion and both peppers, season with salt and cook, stirring occasionally, until the peppers begin to soften, about 5 minutes. Add the corn and scallions, season with cayenne and cook, stirring, until the corn turns bright yellow, about 2 minutes.

3 Add the vinegar mixture to the corn and bring to a simmer. Cook over moderately low heat just until the corn is tender, about 5 minutes. Discard the thyme and tarragon. Season the relish with salt and let cool. Refrigerate for at least 24 hours before serving.

SERVE WITH Grilled chicken, pork or shrimp.

MAKE AHEAD The relish can be refrigerated for up to 2 weeks.

A generous amount of fresh ginger gives this bright tomato jelly its zing.
Great with mild fish, poultry and meats, it makes a lovely gift.

TOMATO-GINGER JELLY

TOTAL 45 min plus 12 hr chilling   **MAKES** 4 half-pint jars

6   medium tomatoes
2   cups white wine vinegar
¾   cup sugar
2   garlic cloves, minced
2   tablespoons minced peeled
      fresh ginger
Kosher salt and freshly
      ground pepper
Low-sugar powdered pectin
      (available at supermarkets;
      see Note)

1 Bring a small saucepan of salted water to a boil. Using a sharp paring knife, score an "X" on the bottoms of the tomatoes. Blanch the tomatoes for 30 seconds, then drain. Slip off the skins and halve the tomatoes crosswise. Remove the seeds and coarsely chop the tomatoes.

2 In a medium saucepan, combine the vinegar and sugar and cook, stirring, until the sugar has dissolved. Add the tomatoes, garlic and ginger and cook over moderate heat for 5 minutes. Season with salt and pepper.

3 Working over a clean saucepan, pass the tomato mixture through a sieve, pressing on the solids. Bring to a boil. Add pectin according to the liquid ratios on the package and boil for 1 minute.

4 Funnel the hot jelly into 4 hot, sterilized jars, leaving about ¼ inch of room on top. Screw on the lids securely. Using canning tongs, lower the jars into a pot of boiling water, making sure they are covered by at least 1 inch of water. Boil for 15 minutes, then transfer the jars to a rack to cool completely. Refrigerate until the jelly has set, at least 12 hours.

SERVE WITH Grilled white fish, roast pork or poached chicken.

NOTE Look for pectin (such as Sure-Jell or Pomona's) that is for use in less- or no-sugar-needed recipes.

MAKE AHEAD The Tomato-Ginger Jelly can be refrigerated for several weeks.

Colicchio served this beloved marmalade with filet mignon when he was chef at New York's Gramercy Tavern. It now appears in the roast turkey, avocado and bacon on ciabatta at his 'wichcraft sandwich shops.

BALSAMIC ONION & GARLIC CONFIT MARMALADE

ACTIVE 30 min   **TOTAL** 1 hr 30 min   **MAKES** about 2 cups

GARLIC CONFIT
6 garlic cloves, peeled
½ cup extra-virgin olive oil

BALSAMIC ONIONS
1 tablespoon peanut or canola oil
4 medium onions, thinly sliced
   lengthwise (about 8 cups)
Kosher salt and freshly
   ground pepper
⅓ cup sugar
⅔ cup balsamic vinegar

1 **MAKE THE GARLIC CONFIT** In a very small saucepan, submerge the garlic in the olive oil and cook over moderate heat until bubbles begin to appear. Reduce the heat to low and cook until the garlic is very soft, about 30 minutes.

2 **MEANWHILE, MAKE THE BALSAMIC ONIONS** In a large skillet, heat the oil until shimmering. Add the onions, season with salt and pepper and cook over moderate heat, stirring occasionally, until the onions are soft, about 20 minutes. Add the sugar and cook over moderately low heat, stirring frequently, until the onions look dry, about 10 minutes. Add the vinegar and cook over low heat, stirring occasionally, until the onions are very soft and dry, about 45 minutes.

3 Stir the garlic confit with its oil into the onions and cook for 5 minutes. Serve warm or at room temperature.

SERVE WITH Grilled rib eye steak.

MAKE AHEAD The marmalade can be refrigerated for up to 2 weeks.

Colicchio's red pepper jelly gets vibrant color from red bell peppers and subtle heat from Fresno chiles. Similar to jalapeños, Fresno chiles turn from green to red as they mature, becoming sweeter and hotter.

RED PEPPER JELLY

ACTIVE 30 min **TOTAL** 1 hr plus 24 hr chilling **MAKES** 3 half-pint jars

3 red bell peppers, minced
3 Fresno chile peppers, minced
1 cup white wine vinegar
⅓ cup sugar
Kosher salt and freshly ground
   black pepper
Low-sugar powdered pectin
   (available at supermarkets;
   see Note)

1 In a large saucepan of salted boiling water, blanch the bell and Fresno chile peppers for about 30 seconds. Drain well. Rinse out the pan.

2 Add the vinegar and sugar to the saucepan and cook over moderate heat, stirring, until the sugar has dissolved. Add the peppers and cook, stirring occasionally, until softened, 5 to 7 minutes. Season with salt and pepper.

3 Add pectin to the pepper mixture according to the liquid ratios on the package and boil for 1 minute. Funnel the hot jelly into 3 hot, sterilized jars, leaving about ¼ inch of room on top. Screw on the lids securely. Using canning tongs, submerge the jars in a pot of boiling water, making sure they are covered by at least 1 inch of water, and boil for 15 minutes. Using the tongs, carefully transfer the jars to a rack to cool completely. Refrigerate until the jelly has set, at least 24 hours.

SERVE WITH Toasts and runny Camembert or any triple-cream cheese.

NOTE Look for pectin (such as Sure-Jell or Pomona's) that is for use in less- or no-sugar-needed recipes.

MAKE AHEAD The jelly can be refrigerated for several weeks.

Debuts as head judge on Bravo's *Top Chef.*

ERIC RIPERT

BEST NEW CHEF '92

Eric Ripert of New York's Le Bernardin is America's most brilliant seafood chef. He sources the best fish, cooking it with astonishing technique or leaving it raw or semi-raw, as its flavors dictate; then he devises deft sauces that reflect his fascination with Latin America, the Caribbean and Asia. A million food fads have come and gone since Ripert arrived at Maguy and Gilbert Le Coze's Le Bernardin in 1991, yet he has continued to stay relevant, grow creatively and maintain the highest standards—a near-impossible feat.

1980 Ripert visits a fortune-teller in the tiny European country of Andorra (where he grew up), who predicts that the 15-year-old will, one day, become a great chef.

This light, easy tuna recipe evokes the flavors of southern France. The fish is crusted with herbes de Provence, then drizzled with Ripert's take on sauce vierge, *an oil that he flavors with sun-dried tomatoes, basil and capers.*

SEARED TUNA WITH SAUCE VIERGE

TOTAL 30 min   **MAKES** 4 first-course servings

SAUCE VIERGE
- 8 drained oil-packed sun-dried tomatoes, minced (¼ cup)
- 2 tablespoons drained capers
- 2 tablespoons finely chopped basil
- 2 tablespoons finely chopped scallion greens
- 1 cup extra-virgin olive oil

TUNA
- Four 4-ounce sushi-grade tuna steaks
- Kosher salt and freshly ground black pepper
- 2 tablespoons herbes de Provence
- 2 tablespoons canola oil
- 1 fennel bulb—trimmed, cored and thinly sliced
- 1 lemon, quartered

PAIR WITH Bright, floral Sicilian white: 2012 Occhipinti SP68 Bianco

1 MAKE THE SAUCE VIERGE Combine all of the ingredients in a small bowl.

2 PREPARE THE TUNA Season the tuna steaks all over with salt, pepper and the herbes de Provence. In a large nonstick skillet, heat the canola oil until shimmering. Add the tuna and sear over high heat until golden, about 30 seconds per side. Transfer the tuna steaks to a cutting board and slice them ¼ inch thick.

3 Arrange the fennel on plates, top with the tuna and drizzle with the *sauce vierge*. Squeeze the lemon over the tuna and serve.

MAKE AHEAD The *sauce vierge* can be refrigerated for up to 6 hours.

Ripert is a master at combining French technique with Asian ingredients. Here, he creates a rich, red wine–ginger sauce and tangy, Thai-inspired mango salad to go with mild baked striped bass.

STRIPED BASS WITH MANGO & PICKLED GINGER SALAD

ACTIVE 40 min   **TOTAL** 1 hr   **MAKES** 4 servings

SAUCE
- 1 tablespoon canola oil
- 3 ounces skinless chicken breast, coarsely chopped
- 5 garlic cloves, sliced
- 2 large shallots, sliced
- One 1-inch piece of fresh ginger, thinly sliced
- 1 tablespoon all-purpose flour
- 2 cups dry red wine
- 3 cups chicken stock or low-sodium broth
- 1 tablespoon unsalted butter, cubed

SALAD
- 2 tablespoons julienned mango
- 1 tablespoon finely chopped tomato
- 1 tablespoon minced red onion
- 1 tablespoon thinly sliced pickled ginger
- 2 teaspoons thinly sliced cilantro
- 2 teaspoons blanched peanuts, chopped (see Note)
- ½ teaspoon fish sauce
- 1 lime, halved

FISH
Four 7-ounce skinless striped bass fillets
Kosher salt and freshly ground black pepper

PAIR WITH Fruit-forward, dry Riesling: 2012 Knebel Trocken

1 MAKE THE SAUCE In a medium saucepan, heat the oil. Add the chicken and cook over moderately high heat, stirring, until browned, about 3 minutes. Add the garlic, shallots and ginger and cook until starting to soften, about 3 minutes. Add the flour and cook, stirring, for 1 minute. Add the wine and simmer until reduced by two-thirds, about 5 minutes. Stir in the chicken stock and simmer until reduced and slightly thickened, about 10 minutes. Whisk in the butter. Strain the sauce through a fine sieve into a small bowl and keep warm. Discard the solids.

2 MAKE THE SALAD In a small bowl, combine the mango, tomato, red onion, pickled ginger, cilantro, peanuts and fish sauce. Season with fresh lime juice.

3 PREPARE THE FISH Preheat the oven to 400° and butter a large baking dish. Season the fish on both sides with salt and pepper. Place the fillets in the baking dish and add 1 cup of water. Bake for about 20 minutes, until a metal skewer inserted in the fish is warm to the touch.

4 To serve, transfer the fish to plates and top with the salad. Drizzle some of the sauce around the fish and pass the rest at the table.

SERVE WITH Red Bhutanese rice or wild rice.

NOTE Blanched peanuts are shelled raw peanuts with the skins removed. They are available at many supermarkets and online at *thenutfactory.com.*

MAKE AHEAD The sauce can be refrigerated overnight. Rewarm gently before serving.

1989 Emigrates from France to the United States to cook for the legendary Jean-Louis Palladin at the Watergate Hotel in Washington, DC.

This beautiful, delicate dish features salmon three ways: fresh and smoked fillets and roe. Ripert gently poaches the fresh fillets for just a few minutes, yielding perfectly rare, incredibly silky fish.

BARELY COOKED SALMON WITH PEA-WASABI PUREE & YUZU BUTTER SAUCE

TOTAL 45 min   **MAKES** 4 servings

1½ cups fresh or thawed frozen peas
1 tablespoon plus 1 teaspoon wasabi paste
Fine sea salt and freshly ground white pepper
2 sticks cold unsalted butter, cut into tablespoons
1 teaspoon finely grated yuzu zest or lime zest
1 tablespoon yuzu juice (see Note)
Pinch of piment d'Espelette
Eight 3-ounce skinless wild Alaskan salmon fillets
4 ounces salmon roe (⅓ cup)
2 ounces smoked salmon, diced (¼ cup)
2 tablespoons finely diced celery
2 teaspoons finely chopped chervil

PAIR WITH Fragrant, lemony Grüner Veltliner: 2012 Hirsch Veltliner #1

1 In a medium saucepan of boiling water, cook the peas until just tender, 5 to 7 minutes. Drain and transfer to a blender. Add the wasabi paste and 6 tablespoons of water and puree until smooth. Season with salt and white pepper. Strain the puree through a fine sieve into a small bowl, cover and keep warm. Discard the solids.

2 In the same saucepan, bring ½ cup of water to a boil. Whisk in the butter, 1 tablespoon at a time, until fully incorporated. Whisk in the yuzu zest, yuzu juice and piment d'Espelette. Season the sauce with salt and white pepper and keep warm.

3 Line a baking sheet with paper towels. In a large skillet, bring 1 cup of lightly salted water to a boil. Season the salmon fillets with salt and white pepper. Place the salmon in the skillet and reduce the heat to low. Cover and cook at a gentle simmer just until the fish is warm to the touch, about 3 minutes. Drain the fish on the prepared baking sheet.

4 Spoon the pea-wasabi puree onto plates and top with the salmon fillets. Drizzle the yuzu butter sauce over the salmon and garnish with the salmon roe, smoked salmon, celery and chervil. Serve immediately.

NOTE If fresh yuzu isn't available, look for bottled yuzu juice at Japanese markets.

This dessert is a clever twist on profiteroles that also happens to be gluten-free. Ripert replaces the usual pastry with fresh, plump apricots, serving them with vanilla ice cream and a warm, spiced chocolate sauce.

SAUTÉED APRICOT "PROFITEROLES"

TOTAL 20 min   **MAKES** 4 servings

APRICOTS

- 3 tablespoons honey
- 1 vanilla bean, seeds scraped
- 4 large, ripe apricots, halved and pitted
- 4 small scoops of vanilla ice cream

CHOCOLATE SAUCE

- 3½ ounces good-quality dark chocolate, chopped
- ¾ cup heavy cream
- 1½ tablespoons honey
- ½ teaspoon cinnamon
- ¼ teaspoon freshly grated nutmeg
- ⅛ teaspoon ground cloves

1 PREPARE THE APRICOTS In a large skillet, combine the honey and vanilla seeds and cook over moderate heat, stirring, for 2 minutes. Add the apricot halves cut side down and cook, moving them frequently in the skillet, until they start to brown, 2 to 3 minutes. Transfer the apricots to a plate.

2 MAKE THE CHOCOLATE SAUCE Put the chocolate in a medium heatproof bowl. In a medium saucepan, combine the cream, honey and spices and bring to a boil. Pour the cream over the chocolate and whisk until smooth.

3 Set 1 apricot half cut side up in each bowl and top with a scoop of ice cream. Set another apricot half on top, cut side down, and drizzle with the warm chocolate sauce. Serve right away.

NANCY OAKES

BEST NEW CHEF '93

Nancy Oakes has an innate understanding of what San Franciscans like to eat, creating big, appealing flavors using French technique, California ingredients and American style. Oakes got her start cooking at a commune, becoming a Best New Chef at Boulevard in the early '90s—a time when female chefs were transforming the food scene in the Bay Area (her peers include Judy Rodgers). Oakes's food still seems fresh and modern, as in a recent dish of ahi tuna tartare with cashew-piquillo hummus and pickled kumquats—sophisticated comfort food from a beloved chef.

*"The quality of the scallops can turn this dish from triumph to tragedy,"
Oakes says. She recommends asking your fishmonger for scallops that
haven't been treated with preservatives. Treated scallops release excess
liquid as they cook and won't develop a tasty crust during pan-searing.*

SEARED SCALLOPS WITH CRANBERRY BEANS, CLAMS & CHORIZO

TOTAL 50 min   **MAKES** 4 servings

2 cups shelled fresh cranberry beans (10 ounces)
1 medium carrot, halved lengthwise
1 celery rib, cut into 3-inch lengths
1 small onion, quartered
1 bay leaf
2 thyme sprigs
¼ cup plus 1 tablespoon extra-virgin olive oil, plus more for drizzling
2 ounces Spanish chorizo, cut into thin matchsticks
¼ cup minced shallots
½ teaspoon minced garlic
¾ cup freshly shucked littleneck clams (from about 2 dozen clams)
1 tablespoon sherry vinegar
½ teaspoon smoked paprika
2 tablespoons finely chopped flat-leaf parsley
Kosher salt and freshly ground black pepper
16 large sea scallops (1½ pounds)
1 cup lightly packed watercress leaves

PAIR WITH Ripe, creamy
Oregon Pinot Gris: 2011
Willamette Valley Vineyards

1 In a large saucepan, combine the beans, carrot, celery, onion, bay leaf and thyme with enough water to cover by 1 inch. Bring to a boil. Cook over moderate heat until the beans are tender and creamy, about 20 minutes. Drain the beans and discard the vegetables and herbs.

2 In a large skillet, heat 3 tablespoons of the olive oil until shimmering. Add the chorizo, shallots and garlic and cook over moderate heat, stirring, until the chorizo fat starts to render and the shallots have softened, about 2 minutes. Add the clams and cook, stirring, until just warmed through, about 2 minutes. Stir in the beans, vinegar and paprika and cook until the beans are hot, about 2 minutes. Remove from the heat and stir in the parsley and 2 tablespoons of water. Season with salt and pepper and keep warm.

3 In a very large skillet, heat the remaining 2 tablespoons of olive oil until shimmering. Season the scallops with salt and pepper, add them to the skillet and cook over moderately high heat until browned on the bottom, about 2 minutes. Turn the scallops over and cook until opaque, about 2 minutes longer. Transfer the scallops to a plate to stop the cooking.

4 Spoon the cranberry beans and clams onto plates and arrange the scallops and watercress on top. Drizzle with olive oil and serve right away.

This salad manages to be both hearty and light, combining strong flavors (beets, arugula, goat cheese) in a bracing lemon dressing. Oakes uses Caña de Cabra, a creamy, soft-ripened goat cheese from Spain, but a semi-firm aged goat cheese would also be good here.

BEET, AVOCADO & ARUGULA SALAD

ACTIVE 25 min   **TOTAL** 1 hr 25 min   **MAKES** 4 to 6 servings

1½ pounds medium beets
¼ cup plus 1 tablespoon extra-virgin olive oil
Kosher salt
¼ cup pine nuts
1 whole lemon
½ teaspoon finely grated lemon zest
2 tablespoons fresh lemon juice
Freshly ground black pepper
2 Hass avocados, peeled and cut into 1-inch pieces
4 cups lightly packed baby arugula
4 ounces Spanish Caña de Cabra, coarsely crumbled, or semi-firm aged goat cheese, shaved (1 cup)

PAIR WITH Elegant, floral Provençal rosé: 2012 Bieler Père et Fils Coteaux d'Aix-en-Provence

1 Preheat the oven to 375°. In a small baking dish, rub the beets all over with 1 tablespoon of the olive oil and season with salt. Add ¼ cup of water, cover with foil and bake for about 1 hour, until the beets are tender. Uncover the dish and let the beets cool slightly. Peel the beets and cut them into 1-inch wedges.

2 Meanwhile, spread the pine nuts in a pie plate and bake for about 7 minutes, until golden. Let cool completely.

3 Using a sharp knife, carefully peel the lemon, removing all of the bitter white pith. Cut in between the membranes to release the sections; cut the sections into small pieces. In a small bowl, whisk the lemon zest and juice with the remaining ¼ cup of olive oil and season with salt and pepper. Stir in the lemon pieces.

4 In a large bowl, toss the avocados and arugula with half of the dressing and season lightly with salt and pepper. Transfer to plates. In the same bowl, toss the beets with the remaining dressing. Spoon the beets over the salad, top with the toasted pine nuts and cheese and serve.

1978 Opens her first kitchen, at the San Francisco waterfront bar Barnacle, where most of the clientele are longshoremen and roadies.

For this fabulous seafood risotto, Oakes folds in Dungeness crab, which is abundant in the Bay Area, but the dish is delicious with any fresh local crab. If oyster mushrooms aren't available, try other varieties, like clamshell, lobster or abalone mushrooms—all are excellent with shellfish.

CRAB RISOTTO WITH OYSTER MUSHROOMS

TOTAL 40 min   **MAKES** 4 to 6 servings

- ¾ **pound oyster mushrooms,** cut into 1½-inch pieces
- ¼ **cup plus 2 tablespoons extra-virgin olive oil**

Kosher salt and freshly ground pepper

- 4 **tablespoons unsalted butter,** cubed
- 3 **cups fish stock or bottled clam juice**
- ½ **medium onion, minced**
- 1½ **cups arborio rice**
- ¼ **cup dry white wine**
- 2 **tablespoons freshly grated Parmigiano-Reggiano cheese,** plus more for serving
- 1 **pound Dungeness or other lump crabmeat, picked over for shells**
- ¼ **cup finely chopped chervil or parsley, for garnish**

PAIR WITH Crisp, full-bodied Chardonnay: 2011 William Fèvre Champs Royaux Chablis

1 Preheat the oven to 375°. On a rimmed baking sheet, toss the mushrooms with 2 tablespoons of the olive oil and season them with salt and pepper. Scatter half of the butter around the mushrooms and roast for 20 to 25 minutes, until they are tender and lightly browned.

2 Meanwhile, in a medium saucepan, combine the fish stock with 2 cups of water and bring to a simmer. Keep warm over very low heat.

3 In a large saucepan, heat the remaining ¼ cup of olive oil. Add the onion and a generous pinch of salt and cook over moderate heat, stirring, until softened, about 3 minutes. Add the rice and cook, stirring, until well coated with oil, about 1 minute. Add the wine and cook, stirring, until absorbed. Add 1 cup of the warm stock and cook, stirring constantly, until nearly absorbed.

Continue adding the warm stock ½ cup at a time, stirring constantly and allowing the stock to be nearly absorbed between additions. The risotto is done when the rice is al dente and suspended in a thick, creamy sauce, about 20 minutes total.

4 Stir the mushrooms, the 2 tablespoons of Parmigiano and the remaining 2 tablespoons of butter into the risotto and season lightly with salt and pepper. Gently fold in the crabmeat; stir in 1 or 2 tablespoons of water if the risotto is too thick. Spoon the risotto into shallow bowls and garnish with the chervil. Pass additional cheese at the table.

Oakes makes this gorgeous risotto with Venere black rice, a naturally black short-grain rice. The glossy grains are especially striking served with the golden butternut squash puree and creamy white burrata.

RISOTTO NERO WITH SQUASH & BURRATA

TOTAL 1 hr 15 min   **MAKES** 4 to 6 servings

1 pound butternut squash—peeled, seeded and cut into 1-inch pieces

1 sage sprig

3 tablespoons unsalted butter

Kosher salt and freshly ground pepper

6 cups chicken stock or low-sodium broth

¼ cup extra-virgin olive oil, plus more for drizzling

½ medium onion, minced

1½ cups Venere black rice (see Note)

¼ cup dry white wine

2 tablespoons freshly grated Parmigiano-Reggiano cheese, plus more for serving

½ pound burrata or fresh buffalo mozzarella, cut into 6 pieces

Flaky sea salt, such as Maldon, for garnish

PAIR WITH Fruit-forward South African Chenin Blanc: 2012 Indaba

1 Preheat the oven to 350°. In a 9-by-13-inch baking dish, combine the squash with the sage sprig, 2 tablespoons of the butter and ¼ cup of water; season with kosher salt and pepper. Roast for about 25 minutes, until the squash is tender and most of the liquid has evaporated. Discard the sage.

2 Transfer the squash to a food processor and let cool slightly. Puree until smooth and season with kosher salt and pepper. Scrape the squash puree into a medium saucepan and keep warm over very low heat.

3 Meanwhile, in another medium saucepan, bring the stock to a simmer. Keep warm over very low heat.

4 In a large saucepan, heat the ¼ cup of olive oil. Add the onion and a generous pinch of kosher salt and cook over moderate heat, stirring, until softened, about 3 minutes. Add the rice and cook, stirring, until well coated with oil, about 1 minute. Add the wine and cook, stirring, until absorbed.

Add 1 cup of the warm stock and cook over moderate heat, stirring constantly, until nearly absorbed. Continue adding the stock ½ cup at a time, stirring constantly and allowing the stock to be nearly absorbed between additions. The risotto is done when the rice is al dente and suspended in a creamy sauce, 35 to 40 minutes total. Stir in the 2 tablespoons of Parmigiano and the remaining 1 tablespoon of butter and season with kosher salt and pepper.

5 Spoon the squash puree into shallow bowls, then spoon the risotto on top and garnish with the burrata. Top with a sprinkle of flaky sea salt and a drizzle of olive oil and serve. Pass additional cheese at the table.

NOTE Venere black rice (*riso Venere*) is a short-grain rice that is less milled and more nutritious than other types of rice. It is available at specialty stores and *amazon.com*.

MICHAEL CORDÚA

BEST NEW CHEF '94

Yucca, *sofrito*, all manner of chiles, live-fire cooking: The Nicaraguan-born chef Michael Cordúa helped introduce now-ubiquitous Latin flavors and cooking methods to the United States at his first Houston restaurant, Churrascos. The recipe pictured on page 77, grilled steak with chimichurri sauce, is his most iconic, though his Amazon chicken breasts, crusted with crushed potato chips and paired with a cilantro sauce, continue to be a favorite on foodandwine.com. These dishes are proof that Cordúa, who now operates seven Houston-area restaurants with his son, David, has a talent for creating delicious flavors that transcend trends.

The extra tang in the ceviche marinade comes from an unexpected ingredient: juice from pickled jalapeños.

RED SNAPPER & SHRIMP CEVICHE

ACTIVE 30 min **TOTAL** 2 hr 30 min **MAKES** 12 servings

½ pound medium shrimp, shelled and deveined

½ cup plus 2 tablespoons fresh lemon juice

½ cup plus 2 tablespoons fresh lime juice

½ cup pickled jalapeño juice (from an 11- to 12-ounce can or jar of pickled jalapeños)

Kosher salt

2 pounds skinless red snapper fillets, sliced into ¼-inch-wide strips

½ small red onion, thinly sliced (1 cup)

2 tablespoons chopped cilantro

1 teaspoon untoasted sesame oil

½ teaspoon sesame seeds

Hass avocado wedges and tortilla chips, for serving

PAIR WITH Spritzy, lime-scented Vinho Verde: 2012 Quinta da Aveleda

1 Fill a bowl with ice water. In a medium saucepan of salted boiling water, cook the shrimp until just white throughout, about 3 minutes. Drain and transfer the shrimp to the ice bath to cool, then drain and halve lengthwise. Transfer the shrimp to a bowl, cover and refrigerate.

2 In a large bowl, mix the lemon juice, lime juice, jalapeño juice and 1 tablespoon of salt. Immerse the snapper in the juices, cover and refrigerate for at least 2 hours and up to 4 hours.

3 Drain the snapper and return it to the bowl. Add the onion, cilantro and shrimp and mix well. Season with salt. Transfer the ceviche to a serving platter and drizzle with the sesame oil. Garnish with the sesame seeds and avocado wedges and serve with tortilla chips.

"In Nicaragua, gallo pinto is the great social equalizer," Cordúa says. "It's part of almost every meal, whether you are rich, poor, white, black or native." He serves this black beans and rice dish to his family for breakfast or a late-night snack, adding crispy bits of fried onions.

GALLO PINTO (BLACK BEANS & RICE)

ACTIVE 30 min   **TOTAL** 1 hr 30 min   **MAKES** 8 servings

1 pound dried black beans, picked over and rinsed

2 garlic cloves, crushed

1 cup Carolina or other long-grain white rice

½ cup plus 2 tablespoons canola oil

1 small white onion, diced (1 cup)

Kosher salt

Chopped cilantro, for garnish

Lime wedges and chopped red onion, for serving

1 In a large saucepan, combine the black beans, garlic and enough water to cover by 3 inches. Bring to a boil and simmer over moderate heat, adding more water as necessary, until the beans are tender, about 1 hour. Drain.

2 Meanwhile, in a medium saucepan, combine the rice and 1¾ cups of water and bring to a boil. Cover and simmer gently over moderately low heat until the water has been absorbed and the rice is tender, about 20 minutes. Transfer the rice to a rimmed baking sheet and refrigerate until cool. (You should have about 4 cups of rice.)

3 In a large skillet, heat ½ cup of the oil. Add the onion and cook, stirring occasionally, until golden, about 5 minutes. Using a slotted spoon, transfer the onion to a small bowl.

Add 3 cups of the beans to the skillet and cook over moderately high heat, stirring frequently, until crispy, about 20 minutes. Stir in another 2 cups of the beans, the cooled rice, the sautéed onion and the remaining 2 tablespoons of oil. Stir to incorporate and season with salt. (Reserve the remaining 1 cup of beans for another use.) Transfer the beans and rice to a serving bowl and garnish with cilantro. Serve with lime wedges and chopped red onion.

MAKE AHEAD The cooked beans can be refrigerated for up to 3 days.

At his restaurants, Cordúa serves a Nicaraguan version of churrasco *(grilled meat), a recipe that originated in Argentina. When Argentinean gauchos in Nicaragua couldn't find the traditional skirt steak, they butterflied tenderloin to mimic the cut. The result is exquisitely tender and flavorful.*

CHURRASCO WITH CHIMICHURRI

ACTIVE 30 min   **TOTAL** 2 hr 30 min   **MAKES** 8 servings

2 bunches of curly parsley (8 ounces), thick stems discarded
⅓ cup garlic cloves, crushed
¾ cup plus 3 tablespoons extra-virgin olive oil
3 tablespoons white wine vinegar
2 pounds trimmed center-cut beef tenderloin
Kosher salt and freshly ground pepper

PAIR WITH Berry-dense, concentrated Syrah: 2010 Barrel 27 Right Hand Man

1 In a food processor, combine the parsley and garlic with ¾ cup of the olive oil and the vinegar; pulse until smooth. Refrigerate the chimichurri for at least 2 hours and up to 8 hours.

2 Using a sharp chef's knife, make a ¼-inch-deep cut down the length of the tenderloin. Turning the tenderloin and rolling it out as you go, spiral-cut the meat until you have a long, rectangular piece that's about ¼ inch thick.

3 Light a grill. Season both sides of the tenderloin with salt and pepper. Rub two-thirds of the chimichurri over the meat and grill over moderately high heat, turning once, for about 4 minutes for medium-rare meat. Let the steak rest for 15 minutes before slicing.

4 Meanwhile, in a small bowl, mix the remaining chimichurri and olive oil. Season with salt and pepper and serve with the steak.

VARIATION In Step 2, cut the tenderloin lengthwise almost all the way through and open it up like a book, about 1½ inches thick. Grill the steak over moderate heat for 7 to 8 minutes per side for medium-rare meat.

According to legend, tres leches *("three milks") cake became popular in Latin America when the Nestlé company printed the recipe on cans of its condensed milk. Cordúa's version is light, supremely moist and topped with billowy swirls of meringue.*

TRES LECHES CAKE

ACTIVE 45 min   **TOTAL** 2 hr plus 2 hr cooling   **MAKES** one 9-inch square cake

CAKE
Unsalted butter, for greasing
1 cup all-purpose flour
1 tablespoon baking powder
4 large eggs, separated
1 cup sugar
¼ cup whole milk
One 14-ounce can sweetened condensed milk
One 12-ounce can evaporated milk
1 cup heavy cream
1 tablespoon pure vanilla extract

MERINGUE
1 cup sugar
4 large egg whites
Pinch of cream of tartar
½ teaspoon pure vanilla extract

PAIR WITH Creamy, caramel-scented Madeira: Blandy's 5-Year-Old Verdelho

1 MAKE THE CAKE Preheat the oven to 300°. Butter a 9-inch square cake pan. In a medium bowl, whisk the flour with the baking powder. In another medium bowl, using a handheld electric mixer, beat the egg whites at medium-high speed until soft peaks form. In a large bowl, beat the egg yolks with the sugar at medium-high speed until pale and thickened, about 3 minutes. At low speed, beat in the whole milk, then beat in the flour mixture. Using a rubber spatula, fold in the beaten egg whites until no white streaks remain.

2 Scrape the batter into the prepared pan and bake in the center of the oven for about 45 minutes, until the top is golden and a toothpick inserted in the center comes out clean. Transfer the pan to a rack and let the cake cool completely, about 2 hours.

3 Using a fork, poke holes all over the cooled cake. In a large bowl, whisk the condensed milk with the evaporated milk, heavy cream and vanilla. Spoon the milk mixture all over the top of the cake, allowing the cake to absorb it before adding more. Let the cake stand for 30 minutes.

4 MEANWHILE, MAKE THE MERINGUE In a small saucepan, combine the sugar with ¼ cup of water and simmer over moderate heat, without stirring, until the syrup reaches 238° on a candy thermometer, about 10 minutes. In a standing mixer fitted with the whisk, beat the egg whites with the cream of tartar at medium speed until foamy. Continue to beat until soft peaks form. Gradually drizzle in the hot syrup and beat at high speed until the meringue just holds stiff, glossy peaks. Beat in the vanilla.

5 Pour off any excess milk from the cake. Invert the cake onto a platter. Swirl the meringue decoratively over the top of the cake. Using a kitchen blowtorch, lightly brown the meringue, then serve.

MAKE AHEAD The cake can be refrigerated for up to 1 day. Make the meringue and finish the cake the day of serving.

2010 Opens his seventh restaurant, a third location of Américas, which spans the cuisines of North, South and Central America.

ANNE QUATRANO

BEST NEW CHEF '95

When she opened Bacchanalia in 1993, Anne Quatrano took on Atlanta's stuffy fine-dining scene, becoming a leader in the New Southern food movement. Much of her success is due to her genius in spotting fantastic ingredients—or, when necessary, growing them herself. She remains one of America's best ingredient scouts, sourcing the most delicious cheeses and produce for the restaurants she runs with her husband, chef Clifford Harrison, which now include Floataway Cafe, Quinones and Abattoir. The superlative Star Provisions market also reflects Quatrano's eye for style and design.

1984 Apprentices with chef Judy Rodgers at Zuni Café in San Francisco; works there for two years.

Ligurian olive oil is ideal in this lovely, light cake because it's more delicate and buttery than many other Italian oils. Fresh fruit and softly whipped cream are perfect accompaniments.

LIGURIAN OLIVE OIL CAKE

ACTIVE 20 min   **TOTAL** 50 min plus cooling   **MAKES** one 10-inch cake

7 tablespoons unsalted butter, melted, plus more for greasing

1¾ cups all-purpose flour, plus more for dusting

1½ teaspoons baking powder

¼ teaspoon salt

¾ cup extra-virgin olive oil

3 tablespoons whole milk, at room temperature

4 large eggs, at room temperature

1 cup sugar

Finely grated zest of 2 lemons or tangerines

1 Preheat the oven to 350°. Butter and flour a 10-inch round cake pan. Into a medium bowl, sift together the 1¾ cups of flour, the baking powder and the salt. In another medium bowl, whisk the melted butter with the olive oil and milk.

2 In a large bowl, using a handheld electric mixer, beat the eggs with the sugar and citrus zest until pale and thickened, about 3 minutes. Alternately beat in the dry and wet ingredients, starting and ending with the dry ingredients. Pour the batter into the prepared pan and bake for about 30 minutes, until the top is golden brown and the side pulls away from the pan. Transfer the cake to a rack and let cool before serving.

MAKE AHEAD The cake can be stored at room temperature for up to 3 days.

Quatrano uses black bass, which she loves for its flaky texture, but snapper, branzino or small cod would also work well in this dish. She simmers the fillets in a broth scented with fresh thyme, fennel and orange zest, then drizzles thick, garlicky aioli on top.

BLACK BASS WITH FENNEL, POTATOES & AIOLI

TOTAL 1 hr   **MAKES** 6 servings

1 large egg plus 3 large egg yolks
1 tablespoon fresh lemon juice
8 garlic cloves, 4 thinly sliced
¾ cup plus 1 tablespoon extra-virgin olive oil
Kosher salt and freshly ground black pepper
4 fingerling potatoes
1 medium onion, diced
1 fennel bulb—trimmed, cored and thinly sliced
6 thyme sprigs
2 fresh bay leaves
Two 2-inch strips of orange zest
Large pinch of crushed red pepper
4 cups chicken stock or low-sodium broth
Six 4-ounce black bass fillets
Croutons, for garnish (optional)
Crusty bread, for serving

PAIR WITH Bright, citrusy Australian Riesling: 2012 Grosset Alea

1 In a food processor, combine the egg, egg yolks, lemon juice and whole garlic cloves and pulse until the garlic is finely chopped. With the machine on, gradually add ¾ cup of the olive oil until emulsified. Season the aioli with salt and black pepper and scrape into a bowl.

2 In a small saucepan of lightly salted boiling water, cook the potatoes until just tender, about 10 minutes. Drain and let cool, then slice ¼ inch thick.

3 In a large cast-iron casserole, heat the remaining 1 tablespoon of oil. Add the onion and fennel and cook over moderate heat, stirring occasionally, until softened, 8 to 10 minutes. Add the sliced garlic and cook, stirring, for 1 minute. Stir in the thyme sprigs, bay leaves, orange zest, crushed red pepper and stock and simmer for 10 minutes. Season with salt and black pepper.

4 Add the fish fillets and potatoes to the casserole and simmer just until the fish is cooked through, 5 to 7 minutes. Discard the bay leaves, thyme sprigs and orange zest. Transfer the fish, broth and vegetables to shallow bowls and garnish with croutons. Drizzle with the aioli and serve with crusty bread.

MAKE AHEAD The aioli can be refrigerated for up to 3 days.

Quatrano has a simple trick for making these duck breasts juicy and flavorful: Just a few hours before pan-roasting, she rubs them with a fresh herb and salt mix, which lightly cures the meat.

SALT-CURED DUCK BREASTS WITH FAVA BEANS & SWEET PEAS

ACTIVE 1 hr   **TOTAL** 5 hr   **MAKES** 8 to 10 servings

Four 1-pound Muscovy or Moulard
    duck breasts, skin scored in
    a crosshatch pattern
2 cups kosher salt
1 cup sugar
1 teaspoon chopped cilantro
1 teaspoon chopped basil
1 garlic clove
1 teaspoon chopped chives,
    plus more for garnish
1 pound fresh fava beans,
    shelled (about 1 cup)
1 pound fresh young peas,
    shelled (1 cup)
1 tablespoon extra-virgin olive oil
4 asparagus spears, thinly sliced
    on the diagonal (1 cup)
2 spring onions or 3 scallions,
    thinly sliced (1 cup)
1 cup chicken stock or
    low-sodium broth
1 cup whole milk
Sea salt and freshly cracked
    black pepper
Chive blossoms (optional) and chervil
    leaves, for garnish

PAIR WITH Spiced, red berry–inflected
Sonoma Pinot Noir: 2011 Banshee
Sonoma County

1 Arrange the duck breasts in a single layer in a glass or ceramic baking dish. In a food processor, pulse the kosher salt with the sugar, cilantro, basil, garlic and 1 teaspoon of chives until finely ground. Rub the salt all over the duck breasts and refrigerate for 4 to 6 hours.

2 Fill a bowl with ice water. In a pot of salted boiling water, cook the fava beans until just tender, 3 to 4 minutes. Using a slotted spoon, transfer the favas to the ice bath. Add the peas to the pot and cook until bright green and tender, 5 to 7 minutes; drain and transfer to the ice bath. Drain the fava beans and peas, then pinch the favas out of their skins; discard the skins.

3 Preheat the oven to 400°. Wipe the curing mixture off the duck breasts. If they have been curing for over 4 hours, rinse them, then pat dry. In a large ovenproof skillet, cook the duck breasts skin side down until golden brown and the fat has rendered, 7 to 8 minutes. Turn the duck breasts skin side up and transfer the skillet to the oven. Roast the duck for about 15 minutes for medium-rare meat; an instant-read thermometer inserted in the thickest part of the breasts should register 135°. Transfer the duck to a cutting board and let rest for 10 minutes.

4 Meanwhile, in a medium saucepan, heat the olive oil. Add the asparagus and cook over moderate heat, stirring, until tender, 5 to 7 minutes. Add the spring onions and cook for 2 minutes, then stir in the fava beans, peas, chicken stock and milk and bring to a simmer. Season with sea salt and black pepper.

5 Thickly slice the duck breasts and arrange in shallow bowls. Spoon the vegetables on top and ladle the broth around the duck. Garnish with chives, chive blossoms and chervil and serve.

"Like all great desserts," says Quatrano, *"these brownies have only three pertinent flavors: chocolate, butter and walnuts."* The brownies bake up thick, giving them a crusty top and rich, gooey middle.

JUMBO BROWNIES

ACTIVE 20 min   **TOTAL** 1 hr 20 min   **MAKES** 12 servings

1 pound unsalted butter

1½ pounds semisweet chocolate, chopped

1 cup all-purpose flour

1 tablespoon baking powder

1 teaspoon salt

6 large eggs

2½ cups sugar

2 tablespoons pure vanilla extract

2 tablespoons strong-brewed espresso

6 ounces semisweet chocolate chips (1 cup)

1 cup walnut halves, lightly toasted and coarsely chopped (optional)

1 Preheat the oven to 350°. Spray a 9-by-13-inch glass or ceramic baking dish with cooking spray. In a double boiler, melt the butter with the chopped chocolate over low heat. In a small bowl, whisk the flour with the baking powder and salt.

2 In a large bowl, using a handheld electric mixer, beat the eggs with the sugar at medium-high speed until pale and thick, 4 minutes. Beat in the vanilla and espresso. Add the flour mixture and beat until just incorporated. Beat in the melted chocolate at medium speed. Using a spoon, stir in the chocolate chips and walnuts.

3 Spread the batter in the prepared baking dish. Bake in the center of the oven for about 1 hour, until the top is shiny and lightly cracked, the edges are set and the center is still a bit jiggly. Transfer the baking dish to a rack and let cool completely. Cut into 12 large rectangles and serve.

MAKE AHEAD The brownies can be stored in an airtight container at room temperature for up to 3 days.

BARBARA LYNCH

BEST NEW CHEF '96

Barbara Lynch began her career as a Todd English protégé, then traveled around Italy learning how to make pasta from *nonnas*. Today she runs a Boston food empire notable for its breadth. There are restaurants: the lovely Italian-French No. 9 Park, the luxe Menton and counter spots Sportello and B&G Oysters. And there's also Drink, one of America's best cocktail bars; The Butcher Shop, which doubles as a wine bar; and Stir, a demo kitchen and cooking school. It's hard to think of another American chef who focuses so hard and well on so many kinds of projects.

1979 Begins first cooking job at the age of 13: preparing meals for priests in the rectory across the street from her home in Boston.

Middle Eastern cooks add the nut-seed mix dukka *to olive oil as a dip for bread. Lynch cleverly sprinkles it onto thin sheets of lavash to fold around asparagus, goat cheese and herb salad like a wrap sandwich.*

TOASTED LAVASH WITH DUKKA & SPRING SALAD

TOTAL 40 min **MAKES** 4 servings

ASPARAGUS
- 1 pound asparagus
- 4 ounces goat cheese, crumbled

LAVASH
- 4 whole wheat lavash wraps or tortillas
- 2 tablespoons extra-virgin olive oil
- 2 tablespoons *dukka* (see Note)

SALAD
- 1 cup parsley leaves
- ½ cup basil leaves
- ½ cup cilantro leaves
- ½ cup chopped chives
- ¼ cup tarragon leaves
- ¼ cup mint leaves
- ¼ cup chervil leaves
- 1 bunch of arugula (about 2 ounces)
- 2 tablespoons extra-virgin olive oil
- 1 tablespoon fresh lemon juice

Kosher salt and freshly ground black pepper

PAIR WITH Brilliant, citrus-spiked Grüner Veltliner: 2012 H.u.M. Hofer Niederösterreich

1 PREPARE THE ASPARAGUS Fill a bowl with ice water. In a medium skillet of lightly salted boiling water, cook the asparagus until just tender, 3 to 4 minutes. Transfer the asparagus to the ice bath to cool, then drain and pat dry; transfer to a platter. Arrange the goat cheese next to the asparagus.

2 MAKE THE LAVASH Heat a large cast-iron skillet. Brush both sides of each lavash wrap with the olive oil and toast in the skillet over low heat until light golden, 1 to 2 minutes per side. Sprinkle with the *dukka,* transfer the wraps to a platter and keep warm.

3 MAKE THE SALAD In a large bowl, combine all of the herbs with the arugula, olive oil and lemon juice. Season with salt and pepper and toss well. Transfer the salad to a bowl. Serve, allowing guests to arrange the asparagus, goat cheese and salad on the lavash.

NOTE *Dukka* is available at Middle Eastern markets and *igourmet.com.*

1983 Her home economics teacher—a master pastry chef—recognizes Lynch's culinary talents and arranges to have her in the class an extra three years.

Lynch's rustic pasta is spicy and satisfying. It's adaptable to whatever summer vegetables are at their peak; here she uses tomatoes, zucchini, summer squash and eggplant.

PASTA WITH CHUNKY TOMATO & SUMMER VEGETABLE SAUCE

TOTAL 1 hr 15 min   **MAKES** 6 to 8 servings

5 tablespoons extra-virgin olive oil
1 small white onion, finely chopped
5 garlic cloves, finely chopped
7 oil-packed anchovy fillets, drained and chopped
2 carrots, cut into ¼-inch dice
2 celery ribs, cut into ¼-inch dice
2 zucchini, cut into ¼-inch dice
1 eggplant, cut into ¼-inch dice
1 summer squash, cut into ¼-inch dice
¾ teaspoon crushed red pepper
Kosher salt and freshly ground black pepper
½ cup dry white wine
5 plum tomatoes, cut into ¼-inch dice
½ cup pitted black olives, coarsely chopped
10 fresh basil leaves
1 pound strozzapreti or other pasta
Freshly shaved Parmigiano-Reggiano cheese, for serving

PAIR WITH Earthy, medium-bodied Chianti Classico: 2009 La Maialina

1 In a large pot, heat 2 tablespoons of the olive oil. Add the onion, garlic and anchovies and cook over moderate heat, stirring occasionally, until starting to soften, 5 minutes. Stir in the carrots and celery and cook, stirring occasionally, until softened, 7 to 8 minutes. Add the zucchini, eggplant, summer squash, crushed red pepper and the remaining 3 tablespoons of olive oil and season with salt and black pepper. Cook, stirring occasionally, until all the vegetables have softened, about 15 minutes. Add the white wine and simmer for 2 minutes. Add the tomatoes, olives and basil leaves and cook, stirring, for 10 minutes. Season with salt and black pepper.

2 Meanwhile, in a large pot of salted boiling water, cook the pasta until al dente. Drain, reserving ½ cup of the pasta cooking water. Add the pasta and cooking water to the vegetables, season with salt and black pepper and cook over moderate heat, tossing, until the pasta is coated. Transfer to a bowl, top with Parmigiano and serve.

MAKE AHEAD The sauce can be refrigerated for up to 2 days.

1987 Shows up two hours late to an interview with chef Todd English and then berates him for choosing a remote location; English admires her spunk and hires her to be the chef at Michaela's in Boston.

*Sometimes served as a special at B&G Oysters or Sportello, this stew
is brimming with shrimp, lobster, clams and scallops. As a garnish, Lynch
bakes croutons with black olive paste; for a shortcut, use olive bread.*

SAFFRON SHELLFISH STEW WITH BLACK OLIVE CROUTONS

TOTAL 1 hr   **MAKES** 6 to 8 servings

CROUTONS
Four ½-inch-thick slices of bakery
    white bread, crusts removed
    and bread cubed
2 tablespoons black olive paste
1 tablespoon extra-virgin olive oil
Kosher salt and freshly ground
    black pepper

STEW
2 tablespoons extra-virgin olive oil
3 garlic cloves, chopped
1 small white onion, cut into
    ¼-inch dice
3 celery ribs, cut into ¼-inch dice
2 carrots, cut into ¼-inch dice
½ teaspoon saffron threads
3 pounds mixed raw shellfish,
    such as scrubbed small clams
    and mussels, scallops and
    shelled and deveined shrimp
½ cup dry white wine
1 pint small cherry tomatoes
1 pound cooked lobster meat
1 teaspoon crushed red pepper
1 tablespoon crème fraîche
Kosher salt and freshly ground
    black pepper
Mixed chopped herbs, such
    as chervil, tarragon, parsley
    and chives, for garnish

PAIR WITH Elegant, berry-scented
rosé: 2012 Commanderie de Peyrassol

1 MAKE THE CROUTONS Preheat the
oven to 325°. In a medium bowl,
combine the bread cubes, black olive
paste and olive oil. Season with salt
and black pepper and toss to
coat. Transfer to a rimmed baking
sheet and bake for 7 to 9 minutes,
until crisp. Let the croutons cool.

2 MAKE THE STEW Heat the olive oil in
a large enameled cast-iron casserole.
Add the garlic, onion, celery and
carrots and cook over moderate heat,
stirring occasionally, until softened,
about 15 minutes. Add the saffron
and stir for 1 minute. Add the clams,
wine and 1½ cups of water and bring
to a boil. Cover and cook until the
clams start to open, about 5 minutes.
Add the mussels, scallops, shrimp

and tomatoes and cook until the shrimp
are almost white throughout. Add the
lobster meat and crushed red pepper
and cook until the lobster is warmed
through, 1 to 2 minutes. Discard any
clams and mussels that do not open.

3 Pour the stew into a large colander set
over a heatproof bowl. Cover to keep
warm. Return the broth to the casserole
and simmer over moderate heat for
2 minutes. Whisk in the crème fraîche
and season with salt and black pepper.
Transfer the seafood stew to a large bowl
and pour the broth on top. Garnish
the stew with the mixed herbs and olive
croutons and serve at once.

To keep the buttery puff pastry base here flat and easy to eat, Lynch bakes it between two cookie sheets until golden and crisp. She then tops the pastry with a gooey dark- and milk-chocolate ganache, fresh fruit and toasted hazelnuts.

PUFF AU CHOCOLAT

ACTIVE 25 min   **TOTAL** 1 hr 30 min   **MAKES** 8 to 10 servings

One 14-ounce package frozen
    all-butter puff pastry, thawed
    and chilled
1 large egg, beaten
Fleur de sel
⅓ cup hazelnuts (about 2 ounces)
5 ounces milk chocolate,
    finely chopped
5 ounces semisweet chocolate,
    finely chopped
¾ cup crème fraîche or
    heavy cream
1 tablespoon rum
1 tablespoon sugar
Fresh raspberries or sliced
    strawberries, for garnish

PAIR WITH Nutty, vanilla-inflected
Madeira: NV Broadbent Rainwater

1 Preheat the oven to 375°. Unfold the puff pastry onto a parchment paper–lined baking sheet. Pierce the pastry all over with a fork, brush with the egg and sprinkle with fleur de sel. Top with another sheet of parchment paper and a second baking sheet. Transfer to the oven and set a heavy ovenproof skillet on the top baking sheet. Bake for 30 minutes, until the pastry is lightly golden and almost cooked through. Remove the skillet, the top baking sheet and the parchment paper and bake for another 20 minutes, until the pastry is cooked through, golden and crisp. Transfer to a rack to cool completely.

2 Meanwhile, spread the hazelnuts in a pie plate and toast in the oven for 6 to 7 minutes, until golden. Let cool slightly, transfer to a clean kitchen towel and rub off the skins. Chop the hazelnuts.

3 In a medium heatproof bowl, combine the chocolates. In a small saucepan, combine the crème fraîche, rum and sugar. Whisk over moderately low heat until simmering, then pour over the chocolate; whisk until smooth. Pour the chocolate evenly over the cooled puff pastry, smoothing the top. Top with raspberries and sprinkle with the toasted hazelnuts and fleur de sel. Cut into pieces and serve.

2010 Opens Menton, an elegant French-Italian restaurant in Boston's Fort Point district.

DANIEL PATTERSON

BEST NEW CHEF '97

Daniel Patterson of San Francisco's Coi is a chef other chefs like to watch. It's a testament to his creativity, influenced by avant-garde methods, classical techniques and naturalist thinking (he's deeply interested in foraging and finding new ingredients in the wild, or even along the side of the road near his house). F&W discovered this self-taught chef in 1997, when he was in his twenties yet cooking with incredible refinement at a little restaurant in Sonoma, long before innovative cuisine had infiltrated that corner of wine country. Today, Patterson is on the short list of global chef superstars.

1988 Works full-time as a cook at Another Thyme in Durham, North Carolina, while attending Duke University.

DEFINING MOMENTS

Sorghum, a type of grass, has seeds that can be popped like popcorn. Patterson tops his nutty, crunchy quinoa salad with popped sorghum, which gives it a buttery flavor. You can also substitute regular popping corn.

QUINOA & CAULIFLOWER SALAD WITH POPPED SORGHUM

TOTAL 50 min **MAKES** 4 servings

1 cup small (1-inch) cauliflower florets
5 tablespoons extra-virgin olive oil
Kosher salt
½ cup red quinoa, rinsed
½ cup white quinoa, rinsed
¼ cup vegetable oil, if popping sorghum
¼ cup popping sorghum, or 2 cups popped sorghum (see Note)
¼ cup roasted almonds, chopped
1 tablespoon minced chives
1 teaspoon unseasoned rice vinegar

PAIR WITH Minerally, medium-bodied Vermentino: 2011 Domaine de Gioielli Cap Corse Blanc

1 Preheat the oven to 350°. On a rimmed baking sheet, drizzle the cauliflower with 1 tablespoon of the olive oil, season with salt and toss to coat. Roast for about 15 minutes, stirring occasionally, until tender and golden brown. Let cool.

2 Meanwhile, bring 2 medium saucepans of lightly salted water to a simmer. Cook the red quinoa and white quinoa separately over moderate heat until tender, 12 to 15 minutes. Drain and rinse under cold running water. Drain well.

3 If popping sorghum, heat the vegetable oil in a medium, heavy pot until almost smoking. Add the sorghum, cover and cook over moderately high heat, shaking the pot occasionally, until the popping has almost stopped; pour into a bowl and season with salt.

4 In a large bowl, combine the cauliflower, red and white quinoa, almonds, chives, rice vinegar and the remaining ¼ cup of olive oil. Season with salt and toss well. Transfer the salad to plates, top with the popped sorghum and serve.

NOTE Both unpopped and popped sorghum are available at *amazon.com*.

MAKE AHEAD The cooked quinoa can be refrigerated for up to 2 days. Bring to room temperature before proceeding.

▶ **1994** Opens Babette in Sonoma, where he is named an F&W Best New Chef; closes the restaurant in 1999 and a year later opens the elegant, French-influenced Elisabeth Daniel in San Francisco (it closes in 2004).

This light, refreshing soup combines sweet red bell peppers with more intensely flavored roasted piquillo peppers. The recipe calls for fresh cranberry beans and green or wax beans, but you can use any combination of shelling and pole beans that are in season.

CHILLED PIQUILLO PEPPER SOUP WITH FRESH BEAN SALAD

TOTAL 1 hr plus 3 hr chilling   **MAKES** 4 servings

6 red bell peppers (about 2 pounds), chopped
One 10-ounce jar piquillo peppers, drained
2½ cups vegetable stock or broth
Kosher salt
1 lime, halved
1 small tomato
4 ounces green beans or yellow wax beans
½ cup shelled fresh cranberry beans
1 tablespoon fresh lemon juice
2 tablespoons fruity extra-virgin olive oil
1 tablespoon chopped mint
1 teaspoon minced preserved lemon (optional)
Freshly ground pepper

1 In a food processor, puree 3 of the bell peppers until smooth. Strain the puree through a fine sieve into a small bowl, pressing on the solids; you should have about 1 cup of pepper juice.

2 In a large saucepan, combine the remaining 3 bell peppers with the piquillo peppers and vegetable stock. Bring to a boil and simmer over moderately high heat until the peppers are tender, about 15 minutes. Transfer to a food processor and puree until smooth. Strain the puree through a fine sieve into a large bowl, pressing on the solids. Add the fresh pepper juice to the bowl and stir to blend. Season the soup with salt and lime juice, cover partially and refrigerate until cold, about 3 hours.

3 Meanwhile, prepare a large bowl of ice water and bring a medium saucepan of water to a boil. Using a sharp paring knife, score an "X" on the bottom of the tomato and blanch in the boiling water for 30 seconds. Using a slotted spoon, transfer the tomato to the ice bath.

Add the green beans to the boiling water and cook until just tender, 3 to 4 minutes; using the slotted spoon, transfer them to the ice bath. Add the cranberry beans to the boiling water and cook until tender, 15 to 20 minutes. Drain the cranberry beans and transfer them to the ice bath.

4 Peel, seed and chop the tomato; transfer to a medium bowl. Cut the green beans into 1-inch pieces and add to the bowl, then add the cranberry beans. Stir in the lemon juice, olive oil, mint and preserved lemon and season the bean salad with salt and freshly ground pepper. Toss to coat.

5 Spoon the bean salad into the center of shallow soup bowls, pour in the chilled piquillo soup and serve.

MAKE AHEAD The soup can be refrigerated overnight.

▲ **2004** Publishes *Aroma: The Magic of Essential Oils in Foods and Fragrance*, co-written with noted perfume maker Mandy Aftel.

This dish was inspired by congee, the smooth porridge that Chinese farmers make from broken grains of rice left over from threshing. Patterson cracks rice in a grain mill, but you can also break the grains in a spice mill or simply purchase broken rice at Asian markets.

SAVORY CHANTERELLE PORRIDGE

ACTIVE 30 min   **TOTAL** 1 hr 15 min   **MAKES** 4 servings

½ cup long-grain rice, preferably Carolina Gold

2½ cups mushroom stock or low-sodium chicken broth

3 tablespoons unsalted butter

1 shallot, minced

1 garlic clove, minced

6 ounces chanterelles or other wild mushrooms, cleaned and cut into small pieces (about 2 cups)

Kosher salt

¼ cup mixed fresh herbs, such as tarragon leaves, chervil and parsley leaves

PAIR WITH Cranberry-scented, aromatic Beaujolais: 2012 Christophe Pacalet Chiroubles

1 In a spice grinder, pulse the rice just until coarsely cracked. In a medium saucepan, combine the cracked rice with 2 cups of the mushroom stock and bring to a slow simmer. Cover and cook over low heat until the stock is absorbed and the rice is tender, about 30 minutes. Remove from the heat and let stand, covered, for at least 5 minutes and up to 30 minutes.

2 In a medium saucepan, cook the butter over moderate heat until golden brown. Add the shallot and garlic and cook over low heat, stirring occasionally, until softened, about 5 minutes. Add the chanterelles and cook over moderate heat, stirring occasionally, until tender, about 5 minutes. Stir in the remaining ½ cup of mushroom stock and the rice and cook, stirring, until the porridge is creamy, about 5 minutes. Season with salt, garnish with the herbs and serve.

Patterson came up with this potato dish one Valentine's Day when he was cooking for his wife, Alexandra. He had a bunch of dandelion greens in the refrigerator and used them instead of the usual parsley to add a slightly bitter edge to a tart salsa verde.

STEAMED NEW POTATOES WITH DANDELION SALSA VERDE

ACTIVE 20 min   **TOTAL** 40 min   **MAKES** 4 servings

1 shallot, minced
2 tablespoons Champagne or white wine vinegar
1 pound small new potatoes
1 bunch of dandelion greens (¾ pound), stems discarded
2 stemmed caperberries or 1 tablespoon drained capers, minced
1 tablespoon fresh lemon juice
½ cup fruity extra-virgin olive oil, plus more for drizzling
Sea salt and freshly ground black pepper
Thinly sliced radishes, for garnish

1 In a medium bowl, combine the minced shallot and Champagne vinegar and let stand for 20 minutes.

2 Meanwhile, in a medium saucepan of boiling water, cook the potatoes until they are tender, about 15 minutes. Drain the potatoes and slice them ⅓ inch thick; keep warm.

3 Prepare a bowl of ice water. In a medium saucepan of salted boiling water, cook the dandelion greens until tender, 7 to 8 minutes. Drain and transfer the greens to the ice bath to cool. Drain and squeeze dry.

4 Finely chop the greens and add them to the bowl with the vinegared shallot. Stir in the minced caperberries, lemon juice and ½ cup of olive oil. Season the dandelion salsa verde with sea salt and black pepper.

5 Spoon some of the dandelion salsa verde onto plates. Top with the warm potato slices and season with sea salt. Garnish with radish slices, drizzle olive oil on top and serve.

MICHAEL SYMON

BEST NEW CHEF '98

Thanks to *Iron Chef* and the talk show *The Chew*, Michael Symon has become one of TV's most visible chefs. He's also one of its most likeable, representing Midwestern integrity and the hometown hero. This Cleveland loyalist (photographed at left with his knife roll) believes in the power of pierogies, like the ones he fills with beef cheeks at his flagship restaurant, Lola—a graceful take on his city's favorite food. Another one of his Midwestern touchstones: the creamed corn with bacon and lime zest on page 118.

1986 At 17 years old, breaks his arm during wrestling practice, which keeps him from competing; to fil his time, he begins cooking part-time at a local barbecue joint.

DEFINING MOMENTS

"This salad is a nod to my mom and my Greek heritage,"
Symon says. In addition to dill, a common herb in Greek
cuisine, Symon adds plenty of mint and basil.

TOMATO SALAD WITH RED ONION, DILL & FETA

TOTAL 30 min   **MAKES** 4 servings

½ red onion, very thinly sliced
   (about 2 ounces)
1 garlic clove, minced
¼ cup red wine vinegar
⅓ cup extra-virgin olive oil
Kosher salt and freshly
   ground pepper
1 red bell pepper, cut
   into 1-inch pieces
One-third of an English cucumber,
   thinly sliced (¼ pound)
¼ cup torn basil leaves
¼ cup coarsely chopped
   mint
¼ cup coarsely chopped fresh dill
1 pound assorted heirloom
   tomatoes, cut into bite-size
   pieces
4 ounces feta cheese, crumbled

1 In a small bowl, cover the onion slices with ice water and let stand for 10 minutes. Drain the onion.

2 In a large bowl, combine the garlic and vinegar. Whisking constantly, drizzle in the olive oil. Season with salt and pepper. Add the bell pepper, cucumber, basil, mint, dill and onion and toss to coat. Let marinate for 15 minutes, stirring occasionally. Add the tomatoes and toss gently; season with salt and pepper. Transfer the salad to a platter, top with the feta and serve.

PAIR WITH Robust, fruit-forward rosé: 2012 De Morgenzon DMZ Cabernet

▶ **1997** Opens Lola in Cleveland's Tremont neighborhood, converting it to Lolita in 2005; reopens Lola in downtown Cleveland in 2006.

"I created this recipe for my father-in-law, who is a big hunter," Symon says. "I'm always looking for ways to cook up his fantastic venison in the fall and winter." In place of the traditional Bolognese combination of beef, veal and pork, the venison gives this lush sauce a great gamey flavor.

CAVATELLI WITH VENISON BOLOGNESE

ACTIVE 30 min **TOTAL** 2 hr **MAKES** 8 servings

- ¼ cup olive oil
- 2 pounds ground venison (see Note)
- Kosher salt and freshly ground pepper
- 1 onion, diced (2 cups)
- 3 garlic cloves, minced
- 2 carrots, finely diced
- 2 celery ribs, finely diced
- 1 cup dry red wine
- One 28-ounce can whole plum tomatoes
- 1 fresh bay leaf
- 6 oregano sprigs
- 2 pounds fresh cavatelli
- ½ cup freshly grated Parmigiano-Reggiano cheese
- 2 tablespoons unsalted butter

PAIR WITH Rich, spicy southern Italian red: 2008 Mastroberardino Radici Taurasi

1 In a large pot, heat 2 tablespoons of the olive oil until shimmering. Add the venison, season with salt and pepper and cook over moderately high heat, stirring occasionally, until browned, 5 to 7 minutes. Transfer the venison to a colander set over a bowl and let drain.

2 Heat the remaining 2 tablespoons of olive oil in the pot. Add the onion and garlic and cook over moderate heat, stirring occasionally, until softened, 7 to 8 minutes. Stir in the carrots and celery and season with salt and pepper. Cook for 5 minutes, then add the wine. Simmer until reduced by half, about 3 minutes. Add the tomatoes, bay leaf, oregano and the drained venison and bring to a simmer. Cover and cook over moderately low heat, stirring occasionally and breaking up the tomatoes, until the venison is very tender and the sauce has thickened, about 1½ hours. Discard the bay leaf and oregano sprigs.

3 Bring a large pot of salted water to a boil. Add the pasta and cook until al dente. Drain, reserving 2 cups of the cooking water. Add the pasta and 1 cup of the cooking water to the Bolognese sauce and simmer over moderate heat, tossing, until the pasta is nicely coated. Add more pasta cooking water if the sauce seems too thick. Remove the pot from the heat and stir in the cheese and butter. Season with salt and serve immediately.

NOTE Ground venison is available at specialty butchers and *localharvest.org.* Alternatively, you can substitute ground lamb for the venison.

MAKE AHEAD The Bolognese sauce can be refrigerated for up to 3 days.

Symon cooks these honey-glazed ribs on the grill from start to finish. Alternatively, you can start them in the oven, then throw them on the grill just before serving for a nice char—or simply cook them entirely in the oven.

GREEK-STYLE PORK SPARERIBS WITH GRILLED LEMONS

ACTIVE 35 min **TOTAL** 3 hr plus overnight curing **MAKES** 4 servings

1 tablespoon coriander seeds
1½ tablespoons garlic salt
1½ tablespoons dried oregano
1 tablespoon smoked paprika
½ tablespoon freshly ground black pepper
½ teaspoon kosher salt
2 racks pork spareribs (about 5 pounds total)
3 tablespoons fresh lemon juice, plus 2 halved lemons
1½ tablespoons honey
2 tablespoons red wine vinegar
1 garlic clove, minced
½ small red onion, minced (about ½ cup)
2 tablespoons extra-virgin olive oil
2 tablespoons chopped fresh oregano
Sea salt, for serving

PAIR WITH Cherry-rich, slightly herbal Greek red: 2010 Skouras Saint George Nemea

1 In a small skillet, toast the coriander seeds over moderately high heat, shaking the pan, until fragrant, 1 to 2 minutes. Transfer to a spice grinder and let cool, then grind to a powder; transfer to a small bowl. Add the garlic salt, oregano, smoked paprika, black pepper and kosher salt and mix well. Rub both racks of spareribs all over with the lemon juice, then rub them all over with the spice mix. Place the pork spareribs on a rack set over a large rimmed baking sheet and refrigerate overnight and up to 1 day.

2 Preheat the oven to 350°. Roast the ribs for 30 minutes, then turn them over and roast for 30 minutes longer.

3 In a small bowl, whisk the honey with the vinegar, garlic and onion. Transfer each rack of ribs to a large sheet of heavy-duty foil and brush with the honey glaze. Wrap up the racks in the foil, seal tightly, then wrap each pack again in foil. Roast the ribs for another hour, until tender. Let rest for 30 minutes in the foil.

4 Light a grill. Grill the halved lemons cut side down over medium-high heat until charred, 2 to 3 minutes. Unwrap the ribs and grill until nicely charred and crisp in spots, about 3 minutes per side (alternatively, broil the ribs 6 inches from the heat). Transfer the ribs to a work surface and cut in between the bones. Arrange the ribs on a serving platter, drizzle with the olive oil and sprinkle with the oregano and sea salt. Serve with the grilled lemons.

MAKE AHEAD The grilled ribs can be refrigerated for up to 2 days. Rewarm before serving.

Lighter than standard creamed corn, Symon's bacon-flecked version gets a little tang from sour cream and a bright kick from lime zest. A simple corn stock made from the cobs boosts the sweet corn flavor.

CREAMED CORN WITH BACON

ACTIVE 40 min   **TOTAL** 1 hr 20 min   **MAKES** 4 to 6 side-dish servings

5 ears of corn—shucked, kernels cut off (5 cups) and cobs reserved

3 garlic cloves, 1 minced

½ onion, cut into 4 wedges, plus 1 cup minced onion

1 tablespoon coriander seeds

1 bay leaf

Kosher salt

1 teaspoon extra-virgin olive oil

¼ pound thick-cut bacon, cut into ¼-inch-thick lardons

½ cup sour cream

1 tablespoon unsalted butter

½ cup chopped cilantro

Finely grated zest of 1 lime

1 In a large pot, combine the corn cobs, whole garlic cloves, onion wedges, coriander seeds, bay leaf, 1 teaspoon of salt and 2 quarts of water. Bring to a boil and simmer briskly until the liquid has reduced to 2 cups, about 30 minutes. Strain the corn stock and discard the solids; keep the corn stock warm.

2 In a large skillet, heat the olive oil. Add the bacon and cook over moderate heat, stirring occasionally, until the fat has rendered and the bacon has browned, about 5 minutes. Add the minced onion and cook for 5 minutes, stirring occasionally. Add the minced garlic and cook for 1 minute. Stir in the corn kernels and 1 teaspoon of salt and cook for 2 minutes. Add the warm corn stock and bring to a simmer. Cook until the stock has reduced to ⅔ cup, about 10 minutes. Add the sour cream and simmer until the sauce begins to thicken, about 5 minutes. Stir in the butter. Remove the skillet from the heat and stir in the chopped cilantro and lime zest. Season the creamed corn with salt and serve warm.

MAKE AHEAD The corn stock can be refrigerated for up to 2 days.

JOHN BESH

BEST NEW CHEF '99

Before Hurricane Katrina, John Besh was simply one of New Orleans's most successful chefs, an ex-Marine with an opulent French-inspired restaurant called August that won him awards. But thanks to his extraordinary post-Katrina efforts to feed relief workers and help his own employees through the crisis, he has come to embody New Orleans and its spirit of resilience. Today, Besh has nine restaurants, all focused on southern Louisiana ingredients and culinary traditions, plus the John Besh Foundation, which is devoted to supporting the New Orleans food community through scholarships, grants and loans.

1977 At nine years old, Besh recognizes his calling to be a chef when he starts cooking for his family after his father becomes a paraplegic in a car accident.

The mingling of oyster juices with butter, herbs, chile and pastis makes these oysters irresistibly slurpable. Besh recommends large, plump varieties like those from the Gulf Coast.

FIRE-GRILLED OYSTERS WITH GREEN GARLIC & PASTIS BUTTER

ACTIVE 20 min **TOTAL** 50 min **MAKES** 2 dozen

2 sticks unsalted butter, at room temperature
¼ cup minced green garlic or scallions
1 teaspoon chopped chives
1 teaspoon chopped thyme
1 teaspoon crushed red pepper
1 teaspoon fresh lemon juice
2 tablespoons pastis or Pernod
2 dozen freshly shucked oysters on the half shell

PAIR WITH Crisp, focused Spanish white: 2011 Lagar de Costa Rías Baixas Albariño

1 In a medium bowl, blend the butter with the green garlic, chives, thyme, crushed red pepper, lemon juice and pastis. Spoon the butter onto a sheet of plastic wrap, roll it into a log and twist the ends to seal. Refrigerate the pastis butter until firm, about 30 minutes.

2 Light a grill. Arrange the shucked oysters on a perforated grill pan and top each with a ¼-inch-thick slice of the pastis butter. Grill the oysters over high heat just until the liquor is bubbling around the edges and the butter has melted, about 3 minutes. Serve the oysters hot.

MAKE AHEAD The pastis butter can be refrigerated for up to 1 week.

"This is my go-to whole roast fish," Besh says. *"It's perfect for summer, when heirloom tomatoes are readily available."* Besh likes to use Gulf red snapper but says that the recipe works with just about any kind of fish.

WHOLE ROAST SNAPPER WITH HEIRLOOM TOMATOES & OLIVES

ACTIVE 20 min   **TOTAL** 1 hr 15 min   **MAKES** 4 to 6 servings

¼ cup extra-virgin olive oil,
    plus more for greasing
One 4-pound whole red snapper,
    cleaned and scaled
Kosher salt and freshly
    ground black pepper
4 garlic cloves, smashed
4 thyme sprigs
1 shallot, thinly sliced
1 orange, thinly sliced
Generous pinch of crushed
    red pepper
1 pint heirloom cherry tomatoes
½ cup pitted olives
1 cup dry white wine
2 chopped scallions, for garnish
Leaves from 2 basil sprigs,
    for garnish

PAIR WITH Fresh, orange-scented Argentinean white: 2012 Kaiken Terroir Series Torrontés

1 Preheat the oven to 450°. Grease a large rimmed baking sheet or roasting pan with olive oil. Using a sharp knife, make ¼-inch-deep slashes on both sides of the fish at 1-inch intervals; transfer to the baking sheet. Season the fish inside and out with salt and black pepper and stuff the cavity with the garlic, thyme, shallot, orange and crushed red pepper. Scatter the tomatoes and olives around the fish, then pour the wine over the tomatoes and olives.

2 Roast the fish until it is golden and cooked through and the tomatoes are nicely charred, about 40 minutes. Transfer the fish to a platter.

3 Add the ¼ cup of olive oil to the baking sheet and toss with the tomatoes and olives. Spoon the tomatoes, olives and sauce over and around the fish, garnish with the scallions and basil and serve.

2001 Opens flagship restaurant, August, in New Orleans, where he prepares regional ingredients in a luxurious French style.

"This recipe is an homage to both my grandmother and my chef mentor Alain Assaud," Besh says. *The fricassee is served over a creamy turnip-rosemary puree, combining American Southern comfort food with the flavors of Provence.*

CHICKEN & WILD MUSHROOM FRICASSEE WITH CREAMY TURNIPS

ACTIVE 1 hr **TOTAL** 2 hr **MAKES** 6 servings

CHICKEN

- ¼ cup olive oil
- 6 chicken thighs with skin

Kosher salt and freshly
    ground black pepper

- 1 onion, chopped
- 1 carrot, chopped
- 1 celery rib, chopped
- 2 garlic cloves, thinly sliced
- 4 ounces wild mushrooms, chopped
- 1 tablespoon tomato paste
- ¼ teaspoon cayenne pepper
- ½ cup dry white wine
- 1 bay leaf
- 2 thyme sprigs
- 4 cups low-sodium chicken broth

TURNIP PUREE

- 4 small turnips (1½ pounds), peeled and quartered
- 1 large Yukon Gold potato (about 8 ounces), peeled and quartered
- 1 rosemary sprig

Kosher salt

- ¼ cup heavy cream
- 6 tablespoons unsalted butter

Freshly ground black pepper

PAIR WITH Earthy, juicy Barbera d'Alba: 2011 De Forville

1 PREPARE THE CHICKEN In a large enameled cast-iron casserole, heat the oil until shimmering. Season the chicken with salt and black pepper. Working in batches, brown the chicken over moderately high heat, 5 to 7 minutes. Transfer the chicken to a plate.

2 Add the onion, carrot and celery to the casserole and cook over moderate heat, stirring occasionally, until lightly browned, 7 to 8 minutes. Add the garlic and mushrooms and cook for 2 minutes. Stir in the tomato paste and cayenne and cook, stirring frequently, until deep mahogany, about 5 minutes. Add the wine, bay leaf and thyme and simmer for 2 minutes. Add the broth and chicken and bring to a boil. Cover and simmer over moderate heat until the chicken is very tender, about 1 hour.

3 MEANWHILE, MAKE THE TURNIP PUREE In a medium saucepan, combine the turnips and potato with the rosemary and enough water to cover by 1 inch. Season with salt and bring to a boil. Simmer the vegetables over moderate heat until tender, 20 to 25 minutes. Drain the vegetables and discard the rosemary. Transfer the turnips and potato to a food processor, add the cream and butter and puree until smooth. Season the turnip puree with salt and pepper and keep warm.

4 Transfer the chicken to a plate. Boil the cooking liquid until thickened and reduced to 2½ cups, about 10 minutes. Discard the bay leaf and thyme. Coarsely shred the chicken and stir it into the reduced sauce; discard the skin and bones. Simmer gently until the chicken is warmed through, about 2 minutes. Serve the chicken fricassee with the creamy turnips.

MAKE AHEAD The fricassee and turnip puree can be refrigerated separately for up to 2 days. Reheat gently.

The French dessert clafoutis is usually made with cherries, but Besh's batter can be used as a base for any fruit in season. "The fruit caramelizes as it bakes and becomes absolutely delectable," he says.

FRESH FIG CLAFOUTIS

ACTIVE 15 min   **TOTAL** 1 hr   **MAKES** 6 servings

2 tablespoons unsalted butter, melted, plus more for greasing

2 cups quartered fresh figs (10 ounces)

1 cup whole milk

3 large eggs

½ cup sugar

1 teaspoon pure vanilla extract

½ cup all-purpose flour

PAIR WITH Dried fruit–scented, caramelly tawny port: Ramos Pinto RP10 10-Year

1 Preheat the oven to 325°. Butter a 10-inch glass pie plate. Arrange the figs cut side up in an even layer in the plate.

2 In a large bowl, whisk the milk with the melted butter, eggs, sugar and vanilla until the sugar has dissolved. Whisk in the flour until the batter is smooth. Pour the batter evenly over the figs and bake for about 40 minutes, until golden and puffed. Let the clafoutis rest for 5 minutes before serving.

2011 Starts the John Besh Foundation, providing grants to help preserve the culinary heritage of New Orleans and Louisiana.

ANDREW CARMELLINI

BEST NEW CHEF '00

New York City chef Andrew Carmellini has an exceptional depth of culinary knowledge that, combined with his drive to achieve perfection, translates into dishes that start trends. Classically trained at Café Boulud in Manhattan, he becomes a student of whatever cuisine captures his imagination: rustic Italian at Locanda Verde, regional American at The Dutch and French in the grand café style at his newest restaurant, Lafayette. Whether he's making lamb-meatball sliders or a sheep's-milk ricotta to spread on toast (two deceptively simple dishes at Locanda Verde), Carmellini has figured out how to make diners care about food they might otherwise take for granted.

1979 At eight years old, makes his way through the *Betty Crocker Cookbook*, baking cakes, cookies and jelly rolls; his grandmother then gives him a copy of *La Méthode* by Jacques Pépin.

These luxurious eggs are a variation on Carmellini's deviled eggs at his restaurant Lafayette. Instead of boiling the eggs, he softly scrambles them to create fluffy, creamy curds. They're amazing on toasted bagels, topped with smoked sablefish, sour cream and briny trout roe.

SOFT-SCRAMBLED EGGS WITH SMOKED SABLEFISH & TROUT ROE

TOTAL 20 min   **MAKES** 2 servings

6 large eggs, beaten
¼ cup plus 2 tablespoons heavy cream
1 tablespoon unsalted butter
Kosher salt
4 ounces smoked sablefish, sliced ¼ inch thick (see Note)
Trout roe (see Note), thinly sliced scallions and sour cream, for garnish
Toasted sesame, everything or plain bagels, for serving

PAIR WITH Fragrant, vivid Chardonnay-based Champagne: NV Pierre Moncuit Hugues de Coulmet Blanc de Blancs Brut

1 In a medium nonstick skillet, combine the beaten eggs with the cream and ½ tablespoon of the butter. Cook the eggs over moderately low heat, stirring them constantly, until small curds form and the eggs are creamy, 5 to 7 minutes. Remove the skillet from the heat.

2 Gently stir the remaining ½ tablespoon of butter into the eggs and season them lightly with salt. Spoon the eggs onto plates and top with the sliced sablefish. Garnish with trout roe, sliced scallions and a dollop of sour cream. Serve right away, with toasted bagels.

NOTE If smoked sablefish and trout roe are unavailable, smoked salmon and salmon roe can be substituted.

This salad is a tribute to Carmellini's former boss, Gray Kunz. The combo of kaffir lime leaf and curry powder in the sauce is "classic Kunz circa the mid-'90s," when they cooked together at Lespinasse in Manhattan. The tangy sauce is also terrific with soft-shell crabs or steamed white fish.

ASPARAGUS SALAD WITH KAFFIR-LIME CURRY & PEANUTS

TOTAL 45 min   **MAKES** 4 servings

1 large egg yolk
2 teaspoons Madras curry powder
2 teaspoons finely grated lime zest
1 fresh kaffir lime leaf, minced (see Note)
¼ cup fresh lime juice
1½ teaspoons minced peeled fresh ginger
1¼ cups grapeseed or vegetable oil
Kosher salt
Cayenne pepper
2 pounds asparagus
1 tablespoon Asian fish sauce
½ small garlic clove, minced
1 small Thai chile, minced
½ teaspoon sugar
1 Fresno chile or jalapeño— halved lengthwise, seeded and thinly sliced crosswise
¼ cup lightly packed torn Thai basil leaves
¼ cup lightly packed torn mint leaves
¼ cup finely chopped unsalted roasted peanuts

PAIR WITH Fruity, minerally northern Italian white: 2012 Alois Lageder Müller Thurgau

1 In a mini processor, combine the egg yolk with the curry powder, lime zest, kaffir lime leaf, 1 tablespoon of the lime juice and 1 teaspoon of the ginger and puree until nearly smooth. With the machine on, gradually add 1 cup of the oil in a very thin stream until emulsified. Season the kaffir-curry sauce with salt and cayenne and scrape into a bowl.

2 Fill a large bowl with ice water. In a large saucepan of salted boiling water, blanch the asparagus until crisp-tender, 2 to 3 minutes. Using tongs, transfer the asparagus to the ice bath to cool, then drain well and blot dry.

3 In another large bowl, whisk the remaining 3 tablespoons of lime juice with the fish sauce, garlic, Thai chile, sugar and the remaining ½ teaspoon of ginger. Gradually whisk in the remaining ¼ cup of oil and season lightly with salt. Add the asparagus, Fresno chile, basil, mint and peanuts and toss well. Season the asparagus salad with salt.

4 Dollop some of the kaffir-curry sauce onto plates, top with the asparagus salad and serve.

NOTE Kaffir lime leaves are the fragrant leaves of kaffir limes, a fruit native to Indonesia, Thailand and other parts of Southeast Asia. They are available at Southeast Asian and some Asian markets and online at *importfood.com*.

MAKE AHEAD The kaffir-curry sauce can be refrigerated overnight.

Garlicky and bright, these crostini are fabulous for entertaining. You can prepare the fava-ricotta pesto in advance and top the toasts just before guests arrive. If you love Parmigiano-Reggiano, follow Carmellini's suggestion to "go heavy with the shaved cheese."

FAVA BEAN CROSTINI WITH PROSCIUTTO & MINT

TOTAL 50 min   **MAKES** 36 crostini

Thirty-six ½-inch-thick diagonal slices of a baguette or small ciabatta loaf
1 tablespoon extra-virgin olive oil, plus more for brushing
1¾ pounds fresh fava beans, shelled
1½ cups fresh ricotta cheese
¼ cup heavy cream
1 small garlic clove, chopped
¼ teaspoon crushed red pepper
¼ cup finely chopped mint
2 tablespoons finely chopped basil
1 tablespoon minced shallot
Kosher salt and freshly ground black pepper
12 thin slices of prosciutto (4 ounces), each cut crosswise into 3 pieces
Freshly shaved Parmigiano-Reggiano cheese and finely grated lemon zest, for garnish

PAIR WITH Clean, citrusy Prosecco: NV Nino Franco Rustico

1 Preheat the broiler or light a grill. On a large rimmed baking sheet, arrange the bread in a single layer and brush both sides with olive oil. Broil the bread 8 inches from the heat or grill, turning once, until lightly browned outside but still slightly soft inside, about 2 minutes.

2 In a large saucepan of salted boiling water, blanch the fava beans until bright green, about 1 minute. Drain and cool under running water. Pinch the fava beans out of their skins and transfer to a bowl. (You should have about 1½ cups of peeled favas.)

3 In a food processor, combine 1 cup of the peeled fava beans with the ricotta cheese, heavy cream, garlic, crushed red pepper and 1 tablespoon of olive oil and pulse until nearly smooth. Scrape the mixture into a bowl and stir in the mint, basil and shallot. Season the fava pesto with salt and black pepper.

4 Spoon some of the fava pesto on each crostini and lay a piece of prosciutto on top. Spoon the remaining ½ cup of peeled fava beans on the crostini, garnish with shaved Parmigiano and grated lemon zest and serve.

MAKE AHEAD The fava pesto can be refrigerated overnight. Bring to room temperature before serving.

1998 Carmellini's grandmother suggests that he should work at Le Cirque after spotting a photo of chef Daniel Boulud in the newspaper; later that year, Carmellini becomes the executive sous chef at Le Cirque.

Carmellini serves this tomato-free take on the classic pasta sauce at Locanda Verde, his modern Italian taverna inside Robert De Niro's Greenwich Hotel. He simmers ground veal and pork in white wine and half-and-half, creating a velvety cream sauce to toss with pappardelle.

PAPPARDELLE WITH WHITE BOLOGNESE

ACTIVE 1 hr   **TOTAL** 3 hr   **MAKES** 2 to 4 servings

3 tablespoons extra-virgin olive oil
1 pound ground veal
½ pound ground pork
½ cup dry white wine
1¼ cups half-and-half
1 cup chicken stock or low-sodium broth
1 thyme sprig
1 small rosemary sprig
2 sage leaves
1 bay leaf
1 small garlic clove, minced
¼ teaspoon freshly ground pink peppercorns (optional)
Pinch of crushed red pepper
Pinch of freshly grated nutmeg
Kosher salt and freshly ground black pepper
¼ cup finely chopped bacon
1 cup finely chopped onion
¼ cup finely chopped white or cremini mushrooms
¼ cup finely chopped peeled celery root
½ pound pappardelle
Freshly grated Parmigiano-Reggiano cheese, for serving

PAIR WITH Juicy, spicy medium-bodied Italian red: 2010 Antinori Peppoli Chianti Classico

1 In a large enameled cast-iron casserole, heat the olive oil until shimmering. Add the veal and pork and cook over moderately high heat, stirring occasionally, until most of the liquid has evaporated and the meat is nearly cooked through, 6 to 8 minutes. Add the wine and cook over moderate heat, scraping up any browned bits from the bottom of the casserole, until evaporated, about 3 minutes.

2 Add the half-and-half and chicken stock to the casserole, then stir in the thyme, rosemary, sage, bay leaf, garlic, pink pepper, crushed red pepper, nutmeg and a generous pinch each of salt and black pepper. Bring just to a simmer. Cover and cook over moderately low heat, stirring occasionally, until the sauce has thickened slightly and the meat is very tender, about 2 hours.

3 Meanwhile, in a medium skillet, cook the bacon over moderate heat, stirring, until the fat has rendered, about 5 minutes. Add the onion, mushrooms and celery root and cook, stirring, until the *soffritto* has softened, about 7 minutes.

4 Stir the *soffritto* into the Bolognese sauce, cover partially and cook over moderately low heat, stirring occasionally, until the sauce has reduced just slightly, about 25 minutes longer. Discard the thyme, rosemary and bay leaf. Season the Bolognese sauce with salt and black pepper and keep warm over very low heat.

5 In a large pot of salted boiling water, cook the pappardelle until al dente. Drain, reserving ¼ cup of the cooking water. Add the pasta and cooking water to the Bolognese sauce and toss over moderate heat until the pasta is well coated, about 2 minutes. Transfer the pasta to a large, shallow bowl and serve right away, passing Parmigiano-Reggiano at the table.

MAKE AHEAD The recipe can be prepared through Step 4 and refrigerated for up to 2 days.

WYLIE DUFRESNE

BEST NEW CHEF '01

Wylie Dufresne of New York City's WD-50 is the face of molecular gastronomy in America. He uses scientific tools and materials to produce witty, complex, often challenging dishes. Some are edible puns, like his Peas 'n' Carrots (the peas are tiny carrot balls in green-pea powder) and Pho Gras, combining a crystalline beef broth clarified in a centrifuge, a round of foie gras terrine and a garnish of sous vide beef tendon fried until crunchy to mimic *chicharrónes*. With Alder, his new spot, he interprets the gastropub trend the Wylie way, offering a clam chowder with oyster crackers made of actual oysters.

1981 The son of a restaurateur, he gets his first job at the age of 11 peeling potatoes in Little Compton, Rhode Island, earning $5 per bucket of potatoes.

Freeze-dried corn is a pet ingredient of Dufresne's. "It has the true sweetness of corn before the sugar converts to starch after the corn is picked," he says. Dufresne uses it to amp up the corn flavor in corn bread, hush puppies and the polenta here, which he fries until crisp outside and creamy within.

DEEP-FRIED FREEZE-DRIED POLENTA

TOTAL 15 min plus 6 hr chilling   **MAKES** 8 servings

6 ounces freeze-dried corn (see Note)
2 cups whole milk
½ teaspoon kosher salt
Vegetable oil, for frying

1 In a food processor, pulse the corn until a powder forms. Transfer to a bowl.

2 In a medium saucepan, bring the milk to a boil. Whisk in the corn powder and salt and simmer over moderate heat, whisking occasionally, until thickened, about 3 minutes. Scrape the polenta into an 8-by-4-inch loaf pan lined with plastic wrap and spread in an even layer. Refrigerate for 6 to 8 hours.

3 In a large, heavy saucepan, heat 2 inches of oil until it reaches 375° on a candy thermometer. Unmold the polenta and discard the plastic wrap. Cut the polenta into eight 1-inch-thick squares or rectangles. Working in batches, fry the polenta, turning once, just until golden, 30 seconds to 1 minute. Drain on paper towels.

SERVE WITH Chicken or duck, or topped with raw fish, cured meats or pickled vegetables as a canapé.

NOTE Freeze-dried corn is available at health-food stores and online at *amazon.com.*

MAKE AHEAD The polenta can be prepared through Step 2 and refrigerated for up to 3 days.

1992 Graduates with a BA in philosophy from Colby College in Maine, then enrolls at NYC's French Culinary Institute (now called the International Culinary Center).

Taking inspiration from the banana curries that are popular in the Caribbean, Dufresne blends banana into tartar sauce, giving it a subtle tropical flavor. He serves the sauce with fried quail at his gastropub, Alder, but says it's also excellent with fried fish or on a chicken sandwich.

BANANA TARTAR SAUCE

TOTAL 15 min   **MAKES** about 2 cups

4   large egg yolks
½   teaspoon whole-grain mustard
1   cup grapeseed or canola oil
2½ tablespoons chopped capers
2½ tablespoons chopped cornichons
1½ tablespoons chopped white anchovy fillets (*alici* or *boquerones;* see Note)
1½ tablespoons chopped parsley
1½ tablespoons chopped tarragon
1   banana, chopped
Kosher salt

In a food processor, blend the egg yolks and mustard with 2 tablespoons of water. With the machine on, drizzle in the oil until emulsified. Transfer to a medium bowl and stir in the capers, cornichons, anchovies, parsley, tarragon and banana. Season the tartar sauce with salt.

SERVE WITH Pan-roasted or fried fish, organ meats or sandwiches.

NOTE White anchovy fillets are available in the deli section of specialty food shops.

MAKE AHEAD The tartar sauce, without the banana, can be refrigerated for up to 1 day. Fold in the chopped banana just before serving.

Dufresne slow-cooks onions with cloves to produce a sweet and fragrant condiment that's great with steak, chicken or shrimp. "Clove has that haunting quality in recipes," he says. "It's there in the background and you try to figure out what it is. I love that."

ONION-CLOVE COMPOTE

TOTAL 1 hr 30 min   **MAKES** 2 cups

2 **tablespoons unsalted butter**
3 **yellow onions (2 pounds), thinly sliced crosswise**
5 **whole cloves**
Kosher salt

In a large, shallow pot, melt the butter. Add the onions and cloves and season with salt. Cook over low heat, stirring frequently, until the onions are very soft but not browned, 1 to 1½ hours. Add water by the tablespoon if the onions get too dry before they're soft. Discard the cloves. Serve warm.

SERVE WITH Grilled steak or shrimp, poultry, sandwiches or soup.

MAKE AHEAD The compote can be refrigerated for up to 1 week.

While experimenting with different liquids to plump up dried dates, Dufresne had an epiphany about root beer. "They both have dark, opulent caramel flavors that play off each other," he says. The sweetness of the compote makes it a natural match for rich meats and oily fish.

ROOT BEER– DATE PUREE

TOTAL 45 min   **MAKES** 2 cups

9 ounces pitted dates
One 12-ounce bottle root beer
Kosher salt

1 In a medium saucepan, combine the dates and half of the root beer. Bring to a simmer and cook over moderately low heat, stirring occasionally, until the dates are very soft, about 40 minutes. Add water by the tablespoon if the dates get too dry before they're soft.

2 Transfer the date mixture to a blender, add the remaining root beer and puree until smooth. Season with salt.

SERVE WITH Roasted pork, lamb or duck or broiled or grilled salmon or mackerel.

MAKE AHEAD The puree can be refrigerated for up to 3 days.

GRANT ACHATZ

BEST NEW CHEF '02

When he opened his Chicago restaurant Alinea in 2005, the modernist chef Grant Achatz redefined the restaurant experience by challenging some very basic conventions of dining. He asked, Why does food have to be just one temperature? It doesn't, he replied, serving a soup called Hot Potato, Cold Potato (page 152). He asked, Why do you have to eat with a fork? You don't, he declared, creating custom-built devices for specific recipes. His fascination with visual surprise and the power of scent makes for thrilling sensory experiences at Alinea, The Aviary cocktail bar and Next, which sells tickets to themed dinners.

"I've always been thrilled by the sensation of having two different temperatures on the palate at one time," Achatz says. Here, he contrasts a creamy, chilled potato soup with hot potato balls.

HOT POTATO, COLD POTATO

TOTAL 1 hr 15 min plus 3 hr chilling   **MAKES** 8 servings

SOUP

- 1 large Yukon Gold potato (about 8 ounces), peeled and cut into ½-inch dice
- ¼ cup black truffle juice (see Note)
- ½ cup plus 2 tablespoons heavy cream
- Kosher salt
- 1 tablespoon white truffle oil

GARNISHES

- 1 pound unsalted butter, plus ½ tablespoon cold unsalted butter cut into 8 very small cubes and frozen
- 1 medium Yukon Gold potato (about 6 ounces), scrubbed and scooped into 8 balls with a ½-inch melon baller
- ½ ounce Parmigiano-Reggiano cheese, cut into 8 very small pieces
- 2 chives, cut into eight 1-inch lengths
- 8 thin slices of fresh black truffle (optional)
- Maldon salt

1 MAKE THE SOUP In a small saucepan, combine the diced potato with the truffle juice and bring to a boil. Cover and simmer over low heat until the potato is tender, about 20 minutes. Add the cream and return to a simmer.

2 Transfer the potato mixture to a blender. Add ¾ teaspoon of salt and ⅓ cup of water and puree until smooth. With the machine on, drizzle in the truffle oil until incorporated. Season with salt. Strain the soup through a fine sieve into a medium bowl. Cover and refrigerate until thoroughly chilled, about 3 hours.

3 PREPARE THE GARNISHES In a medium saucepan, melt the pound of butter. Simmer gently over low heat until foam rises to the surface, about 3 minutes. Using a spoon, skim the foam off the surface. Slowly pour the butter through a cheesecloth-lined sieve into a medium bowl, stopping before you reach the milky solids at the bottom of the saucepan; wipe out the pan. Return the clarified butter to the saucepan and add the potato balls. Bring to a slow simmer over moderately low heat and cook the potato balls until they are tender, about 15 minutes. Keep the potato balls in the butter.

4 Pour the chilled soup into 8 small bowls or shot glasses. Garnish each soup with 1 piece of cheese, frozen butter and chive, plus a hot potato ball and a truffle slice. Sprinkle with Maldon salt and serve. Alternatively, skewer 1 piece of cheese, frozen butter and chive and a hot potato ball onto each of 8 mini skewers, drape with a truffle slice, sprinkle with Maldon salt and serve.

NOTE Black truffle juice is available at Italian specialty stores and online at *amazon.com*.

MAKE AHEAD The potato soup can be refrigerated for up to 2 days.

This play on the classic sandwich is brilliant and simple. It features neither peanut butter nor jelly but tastes just like the familiar combination. Achatz seasons green grapes with a sherry vinegar that's been aged for 18 years, making it syrupy and super-intense.

PB&J CANAPÉS

TOTAL 25 min   **MAKES** 6 servings

16   green grapes, peeled
 1   teaspoon minced tarragon
 ¼   teaspoon Blis Elixir vinegar
     (see Note)
Freshly ground pepper
12   thin baguette slices
 1   tablespoon roasted peanut oil
Maldon salt, for serving

PAIR WITH Juicy sparkling rosé: NV Scharffenberger Brut Excellence

1 Preheat the oven to 325°. In a small bowl, using a fork, crush the peeled grapes. Stir in the minced tarragon and vinegar. Season with pepper.

2 Brush the baguette slices with the peanut oil and toast in the oven for 8 to 10 minutes, until crisp. Top the toasts with the crushed grapes, sprinkle with Maldon salt and serve.

NOTE Blis Elixir is a brand of aged sherry vinegar. It's available at *blisgourmet.com.*

▲ **2000** Has a revelatory experience working at Ferran Adrià's El Bulli, the (now closed) restaurant in Roses, Spain, that helped pioneer the molecular gastronomy movement.

Inspired by a Southern sweet potato pie, these genius bite-size desserts have a sweet potato custard filling in a crunchy tempura shell. Achatz serves them with two coatings—cinnamon sugar and brown-sugar-and-salt—along with shots of bourbon.

SWEET POTATO, BROWN SUGAR, BOURBON

ACTIVE 30 min **TOTAL** 1 hr **MAKES** 6 to 8 servings

1 large sweet potato (about 8 ounces), peeled and cut into 1-inch dice
Kosher salt
Ten 3-inch cinnamon sticks (1 ounce)
¼ cup granulated sugar
1½ tablespoons light brown sugar
Canola oil, for frying
1 cup plus 2 tablespoons all-purpose flour
1 tablespoon baking powder
1 tablespoon cornstarch
½ cup well-chilled seltzer or club soda
6 to 8 shots of bourbon, for serving

1 Preheat the oven to 350°. On a rimmed baking sheet, spread the sweet potato cubes in an even layer and season with salt. Roast until almost tender, about 30 minutes. Let the sweet potato cool.

2 Meanwhile, in an ovenproof skillet, bake the cinnamon sticks until fragrant, about 10 minutes. Crush the cinnamon sticks, transfer to a blender and blend until a fine powder forms. Sift the cinnamon powder through a fine sieve into a small bowl, then stir in the granulated sugar and 1 teaspoon of salt. In another small bowl, stir the brown sugar with 1½ tablespoons of salt.

3 In a medium, heavy saucepan, heat 2 inches of oil until it reaches 375° on a candy thermometer. Line a baking sheet with paper towels. In a small bowl, whisk ½ cup plus 2 tablespoons of the flour with the baking powder and cornstarch.

Transfer ½ cup of the dry ingredients to a medium bowl, then whisk in the seltzer just until smooth. (Discard the rest of the dry ingredients.) Place the remaining ½ cup of flour in a small bowl.

4 Working in batches, toss the sweet potato cubes in the flour and tap off the excess. Using a fork, dip the cubes in the tempura batter, allowing the excess to drip back into the bowl. Add the battered sweet potato cubes to the hot oil and fry until golden, about 3 minutes per batch. Drain on the paper towels. Serve the sweet potato tempura with the two sugars for dipping and shots of bourbon on the side.

MAKE AHEAD The roasted sweet potato cubes can be refrigerated for up to 2 days. Bring them to room temperature before proceeding.

▶ **2005** Opens Alinea in Chicago, offering guests ambitious 18-course tasting menus.

Nostalgic for the caramel popcorn he loved as a kid, Achatz captures the flavor in the brilliant warm dessert drink he serves at Alinea. It has two parts: a rich, buttery popcorn broth and a frothy, light caramel topping.

CARAMEL POPCORN SHOOTERS

ACTIVE 30 min   **TOTAL** 1 hr   **MAKES** 8 to 10 servings

CARAMEL FROTH
1 cup plus 2 tablespoons sugar
2 teaspoons soy lecithin powder (see Note)

POPCORN BROTH
2 tablespoons canola oil
½ cup popping corn
2 teaspoons kosher salt
7 tablespoons unsalted butter
¼ cup plus 1 tablespoon sugar

1 **MAKE THE CARAMEL FROTH** In a small saucepan, combine 2 tablespoons of the sugar with 2 tablespoons of water and simmer the syrup over moderate heat just until the sugar has dissolved.

2 In another small saucepan, combine the remaining 1 cup of sugar with ½ cup of water and simmer over moderate heat, without stirring, until an amber caramel forms (340° on a candy thermometer), about 15 minutes. Immediately add ⅓ cup of water and the sugar syrup; be careful, as the caramel mixture will bubble and splatter. Whisk until smooth, then transfer the caramel syrup to a medium bowl and let stand for 30 minutes.

3 **MEANWHILE, MAKE THE POPCORN BROTH** In a large, heavy saucepan, heat the canola oil until just smoking. Add the popping corn, cover and cook over moderately high heat, shaking the pan constantly, until the kernels have stopped popping, 2 to 3 minutes.

4 In another large saucepan, combine the popcorn with the salt, butter, sugar and 3½ cups of water. Bring to a simmer and cook over moderate heat for 5 minutes. Strain the broth through a fine sieve into a bowl, pressing on the popcorn until only the kernels remain; discard the kernels.

5 Transfer the popcorn broth to a blender and blend until frothy, about 3 minutes. Add the lecithin powder to the caramel syrup and blend with an immersion blender until frothy.

6 Pour the warm popcorn broth into small glasses, filling them halfway (about ¼ cup each). Spoon some of the caramel froth on top and serve.

NOTE Soy lecithin powder is available at health-food stores and online at *amazon.com.*

MAKE AHEAD The popcorn broth can be refrigerated for up to 2 days. Reheat and froth in the blender just before serving.

STUART BRIOZA

BEST NEW CHEF '03

03

Stuart Brioza has a sixth sense for finding the deliciousness in every kind of food he makes. At the idiosyncratic State Bird Provisions in San Francisco, he brings a freewheeling American attitude to the Chinese dim sum experience, serving globally inflected small plates, both from a menu and from roving carts. Dishes like guinea hen dumplings in broth and raw oysters with spicy kohlrabi are quiet works of genius. Next up for Brioza and his pastry-chef wife, Nicole Krasinski: The Progress, which is due to open in 2014 in the same turn-of-the-century building that houses State Bird.

1989 At 15 years old, skips classes to take a cleaning job at a local Italian restaurant in Cupertino, California; soon moves on to making fresh pastas and sauces.

Brioza's corn pancakes are puffy in the center and crispy at the edges, with lots of crunchy corn inside and melted cheese on top. He loves Mt. Tam, a triple-cream cow's-milk cheese from California's Cowgirl Creamery; St. André is delicious here, too.

SWEET CORN PANCAKES WITH MT. TAM CHEESE

TOTAL 35 min   **MAKES** 4 to 6 first-course servings

3 large ears of corn, shucked
1 large egg, lightly beaten
1½ cups all-purpose flour
1½ teaspoons salt
1 teaspoon baking powder
½ cup finely chopped scallions
¼ cup canola oil,
    plus more as needed
2 ounces Cowgirl Creamery's
    Mt. Tam or other triple-cream
    cheese, such as St. André,
    cut into ½-inch wedges
Freshly ground black pepper

PAIR WITH Ripe, full-bodied
California Chardonnay:
2011 St. Francis Sonoma County

1 In a large saucepan of salted boiling water, cook the corn until crisp-tender, 3 to 5 minutes. Transfer the corn to a plate and let cool completely, then cut the kernels off the cobs.

2 In a large bowl, beat the egg with 1¼ cups of water. Sift the flour, salt and baking powder over the egg and whisk until a batter forms. Stir in the corn kernels and scallions.

3 In a large nonstick skillet, heat the ¼ cup of canola oil until shimmering. Spoon a scant ¼ cup of the batter into the skillet for each pancake and cook over moderate heat until browned on the bottom, 1 to 2 minutes. Flip the pancakes and top each with a piece of cheese. Cook until the cheese just starts to melt and the pancakes are cooked through, about 2 minutes longer. Transfer the pancakes to a platter and season with black pepper. Serve warm.

MAKE AHEAD The pancake batter can be refrigerated overnight. Stir in the corn and scallions just before cooking.

▶ **1992** Enrolls at De Anza College in Cupertino, where he meets his future wife and pastry chef, Nicole Krasinski.

This revamp of the Chinese takeout staple gets heat from jalapeño peppers and tartness from fresh lime juice. The broth, infused with ginger, lemongrass and kaffir lime leaves, is pureed with yellow-eyed peas, giving the soup a buttery richness.

HOT & SOUR YELLOW-EYED PEA SOUP WITH CHICKEN

ACTIVE 1 hr   **TOTAL** 2 hr plus overnight soaking   **MAKES** 4 to 6 servings

2 cups dried yellow-eyed peas, soaked overnight and drained

Kosher salt

One 3-pound chicken, quartered and skin discarded

4 cups chicken stock or low-sodium broth

1 lemongrass stalk, cut into 2-inch pieces and lightly crushed

2 fresh kaffir lime leaves (see Note)

One 3-inch piece of peeled fresh ginger (3 ounces)—2 inches crushed, 1 inch thinly sliced

6 garlic cloves, crushed

1 cup lightly packed cilantro leaves, plus more for serving

1 cup lightly packed mint leaves, plus more for serving

2 tablespoons Asian fish sauce, preferably Red Boat

1 small jalapeño, thinly sliced, plus thin slices for serving

4 tablespoons unsalted butter

¼ cup fresh lime juice, plus lime wedges for serving

Thinly sliced radishes, for serving

1 In a large saucepan, cover the yellow-eyed peas with water and bring to a boil. Simmer over low heat until tender, 35 to 40 minutes. Remove from the heat, add a generous pinch of salt and let stand for 10 minutes. Drain and spread the peas on a baking sheet to cool.

2 Meanwhile, in a large pot, combine the chicken, chicken stock, lemongrass, lime leaves, crushed ginger, 4 of the garlic cloves and 4 cups of water and bring to a boil. Simmer over moderately low heat, skimming the surface as necessary, until the chicken is cooked and the broth is flavorful, about 40 minutes. Remove from the heat and stir in the 1 cup each of cilantro and mint, the fish sauce and jalapeño and let stand for 20 minutes.

3 Transfer the chicken to a plate to cool. Strain the broth through a fine sieve into a large heatproof bowl; discard the aromatics and herbs. Wipe out the pot.

4 Melt the butter in the pot. Add the sliced ginger and the remaining 2 garlic cloves and cook over moderate heat, stirring, until fragrant, about 2 minutes. Stir in half of the cooked yellow-eyed peas and the chicken broth and bring just to a boil, then remove from the heat.

5 Working in batches, carefully puree the soup in a blender until smooth. Return the soup to the pot and bring just to a simmer. Remove the chicken from the bones and shred the meat. Stir the shredded chicken, lime juice and the remaining yellow-eyed peas into the soup and season lightly with salt. Ladle the soup into bowls and serve with cilantro and mint leaves, jalapeño and radish slices and lime wedges.

NOTE Kaffir lime leaves are the fragrant leaves of kaffir limes, a fruit native to Indonesia, Thailand and other parts of Southeast Asia. They are available at Southeast Asian and some Asian markets and online at *importfood.com.*

MAKE AHEAD The soup can be refrigerated overnight. Reheat gently and garnish just before serving.

▶ **1998** Cooks at Michel Rostang in Paris, immersing himself in French culinary technique; gets first chef job two years later at Tapawingo (now closed) in Ellsworth, Michigan, where he's named a Best New Chef in 2003.

*The key to the flaky, super-crisp texture of these crackers
is pastry flour, a low-protein, low-gluten flour.*

ROSEMARY-BUTTERMILK CRACKERS WITH CHANTERELLE SPREAD

ACTIVE 1 hr 15 min   **TOTAL** 2 hr plus 3 hr chilling   **MAKES** four 10-inch crackers

CRACKERS

2½ cups pastry flour,
  plus more for dusting
1 tablespoon sugar
½ teaspoon baking powder
½ teaspoon kosher salt
1 stick cold unsalted butter, cubed
1 cup buttermilk
Extra-virgin olive oil, for brushing
Rosemary leaves, coarse sea salt
  and freshly ground pepper,
  for sprinkling

CHANTERELLE SPREAD

1 stick unsalted butter
2 medium shallots, minced
1 large garlic clove, minced
1 small rosemary sprig
¼ pound chanterelle mushrooms,
  wiped clean and cut into
  1-inch pieces
Kosher salt and freshly
  ground pepper
¼ cup Madeira
1 cup chicken stock or
  low-sodium broth
½ cup cream cheese, softened
¾ ounce Pecorino Fiore Sardo
  cheese, finely grated
Tabasco

PAIR WITH Full-bodied, stony
Chablis: 2012 Patrick Piuze Terroirs
de Courgis

1 MAKE THE CRACKER DOUGH In a food processor, pulse the 2½ cups of flour with the sugar, baking powder and kosher salt. Scatter the butter on top and pulse until a coarse meal forms. Transfer to a large bowl and make a well in the center. Pour in the buttermilk and, using your hands, gradually mix until a soft dough forms. Scrape the dough onto a lightly floured work surface and knead gently just until smooth. Divide the dough into 4 pieces and shape into disks; wrap in plastic and refrigerate for at least 3 hours or overnight.

2 MEANWHILE, MAKE THE CHANTERELLE SPREAD In a large skillet, melt the butter over moderately low heat. Add the shallots, garlic and rosemary and cook over moderately high heat, stirring, until the butter is golden, about 5 minutes. Add the chanterelles and a pinch each of salt and pepper and cook, stirring occasionally, until softened, about 5 minutes. Add the Madeira and stock and bring to a boil. Simmer over moderate heat, stirring occasionally, until the liquid has reduced by half, about 7 minutes. Discard the rosemary sprig.

3 Scrape the mushroom mixture into a food processor and let cool slightly. Add the cream cheese and pecorino and puree until smooth. Season with salt, pepper and Tabasco and let cool.

4 BAKE THE CRACKERS Preheat the oven to 375° and line 2 baking sheets with parchment paper. On a floured work surface, dust 1 disk of the cracker dough with flour. Roll out the dough to a 10-inch-long oval a scant ⅛ inch thick and transfer it to a prepared baking sheet. Repeat with 1 more disk of dough. Brush the dough with olive oil and sprinkle with rosemary, coarse sea salt and pepper.

5 Bake the crackers for about 18 minutes, until crisp; shift the baking sheets from top to bottom and front to back halfway through. Transfer the crackers to racks to cool completely. Repeat with the remaining 2 disks of dough. Serve the crackers with the chanterelle spread.

MAKE AHEAD The crackers can be stored in an airtight container at room temperature for up to 3 days. The chanterelle spread can be refrigerated for up to 3 days.

This meal-in-one recipe is a more wholesome take on pork fried rice. Instead of stirring in the usual scrambled egg, Brioza tops the dish with an oozy poached egg.

SAUSAGE FRIED FARRO WITH SHIITAKE, RADISHES & SCALLIONS

ACTIVE 35 min   **TOTAL** 55 min   **MAKES** 4 servings

1 cup semi-pearled farro
1 large rosemary sprig
1 garlic clove, crushed
Kosher salt
⅓ cup plus 2 tablespoons extra-virgin olive oil
10 ounces spicy Italian sausage, casings removed and sausage crumbled
¼ pound shiitake mushrooms, stems discarded and caps cut into 1-inch pieces
8 medium radishes, quartered (1 cup)
¾ cup thinly sliced scallions
½ cup chopped parsley
Freshly ground pepper
4 large eggs

PAIR WITH Concentrated, ripe-fruited Sonoma white: 2012 Wind Gap Trousseau Gris

1 Bring a large saucepan of water to a boil. Add the farro, rosemary, garlic, a generous pinch of salt and 2 tablespoons of the olive oil and simmer over moderate heat until the farro is tender, 20 to 25 minutes. Drain the farro and spread on a baking sheet to cool; discard the rosemary and garlic.

2 In a large skillet, heat the remaining ⅓ cup of olive oil until shimmering. Add the sausage and cook over moderate heat, breaking the meat into pieces, until it starts to brown, about 4 minutes. Add the shiitake and cook, stirring, until just tender, about 3 minutes. Stir in the farro, radishes and scallions and cook, stirring, until the farro is coated and the radishes are crisp-tender, about 5 minutes. Remove from the heat. Stir in the parsley and season with salt and pepper; keep warm.

3 Fill a large, deep skillet with water and bring just to a simmer. One at a time, crack the eggs into the simmering water. Poach the eggs until the whites are set and the yolks are runny, about 4 minutes. Using a slotted spoon, transfer the eggs to a paper towel–lined plate and season with salt and pepper. To serve, spoon the sausage fried farro into shallow bowls and top with the eggs.

GRAHAM ELLIOT

BEST NEW CHEF '04

04

A lobster corn dog: It's the dish Graham Elliot makes every year as the culinary director for the Lollapalooza music festival in Chicago, and also a recipe that shows his whimsical high-low style. When he isn't pumping up Lollapalooza's food cred by selecting extraordinary vendors or running his own sandwich joint, Grahamwich, the Charlie Trotter protégé oversees the Michelin-starred Graham Elliot and his bistro, G.E.B. The recipes that follow show how well his cooking translates to the home kitchen.

1994 ► Works as a dishwasher and busboy at Chix café in Virginia Beach; a year later, drops out of high school and starts culinary school at Johnson & Wales in Norfolk, Virginia.

This play on split pea soup gets its vibrant flavor from just-shucked peas and fennel. Even made with frozen peas, the soup tastes surprisingly fresh. Instead of simmering ham hocks in the broth, Elliot garnishes the soup with a spoonful of smoky ham salad and baby greens.

FRESH PEA SOUP WITH HAM

TOTAL 45 min   **MAKES** 4 servings

1 tablespoon unsalted butter
1 small fennel bulb—trimmed, cored and thinly sliced (¾ cup)
½ medium onion, thinly sliced (1¼ cups)
2 garlic cloves, chopped
Kosher salt
1 quart whole milk
4 cups shelled fresh or thawed frozen peas (about 1 pound)
½ cup diced smoked ham hock (from one 11-ounce ham hock) or smoky ham
1 tablespoon minced shallot
½ tablespoon chopped chives
1 teaspoon extra-virgin olive oil
½ teaspoon sherry vinegar
Pea tendrils or baby arugula, for garnish

PAIR WITH Vibrant, citrusy Pinot Grigio: 2012 Kris

1 In a large pot, melt the butter. Add the fennel, onion and garlic and season with salt. Cook the vegetables over moderate heat, stirring, until they are tender but not browned, 8 to 10 minutes. Add the milk and simmer for 15 minutes. Add the peas and simmer until tender, 7 to 8 minutes.

2 Working in batches, puree the soup in a blender, then strain through a fine sieve into a large bowl. Season the soup with salt.

3 In a small bowl, combine the diced ham with the shallot, chives, olive oil and sherry vinegar. Spoon the ham salad into 4 bowls. Ladle the warm pea soup into the bowls, garnish with pea tendrils and serve immediately.

At G.E.B., his eclectic Chicago bistro, Elliot creates casual dishes that usually feature just three main components. For this very simple salad, he updates a classic combination of roasted beets and arugula by adding burrata (cream-filled mozzarella) marinated in olive oil and herbs.

BEET & ARUGULA SALAD WITH MARINATED BURRATA

ACTIVE 30 min   **TOTAL** 1 hr   **MAKES** 4 servings

8 ounces burrata (see Note)
½ teaspoon fenugreek seeds
½ teaspoon black peppercorns
½ cup plus 1 tablespoon extra-virgin olive oil
5 thyme sprigs
1 pound baby beets
4 fresh bay leaves
1 tablespoon white wine vinegar
Kosher salt
20 arugula leaves
Juice and finely grated zest of 1 lemon
Fleur de sel, for serving
Freshly cracked pepper, for serving

1 Preheat the oven to 400°. Place the burrata in a small bowl. In a small saucepan, toast the fenugreek seeds and peppercorns over moderately low heat until fragrant, 2 to 3 minutes. Add ¼ cup of the olive oil and 3 of the thyme sprigs and bring to a bare simmer; simmer gently for 3 minutes. Let cool until lukewarm, then pour the infused oil over the burrata. Let the burrata marinate for 1 hour. Discard the aromatics.

2 Meanwhile, in a small roasting pan lined with foil, combine the beets with the bay leaves, vinegar, 2 teaspoons of salt, ½ cup of water, 1 tablespoon of the olive oil and the remaining 2 thyme sprigs. Cover with foil and roast until the beets are tender, about 30 minutes. Uncover and let cool briefly. Peel the beets and cut them into bite-size wedges. In a small bowl, toss the beets with 1 tablespoon of the olive oil and season with salt.

3 In a medium bowl, toss the arugula with 1 tablespoon of the olive oil and season with lemon juice. Arrange the beets on plates. Tear the burrata into pieces and set them beside the beets. Top with the arugula and lemon zest. Sprinkle the salads with fleur de sel and cracked pepper, drizzle with the remaining 2 tablespoons of olive oil and serve.

NOTE If you can't find burrata, buffalo mozzarella is a fine substitute.

MAKE AHEAD The roasted beets can be refrigerated for up to 2 days. Bring to room temperature before serving.

To achieve super-juicy white meat, Elliot sears the chicken breasts with the skin on, then bastes them with a garlicky thyme butter.

CHICKEN WITH GREEN BEANS IN BUTTERMILK-TARRAGON DRESSING

TOTAL 50 min   **MAKES** 4 servings

10 ounces green beans
¼ cup plain whole-milk
   Greek yogurt
¼ cup buttermilk
1 teaspoon Dijon mustard
1 teaspoon fresh lemon juice
2 tablespoons chopped tarragon
Kosher salt
1 tablespoon olive oil
4 boneless chicken breasts
   with skin
Freshly ground pepper
2 tablespoons unsalted butter
2 thyme sprigs
1 garlic clove, lightly crushed

PAIR WITH Citrusy, apple-scented Chenin Blanc: 2011 Champalou Vouvray

1 Preheat the oven to 350°. Prepare a bowl of ice water. In a medium saucepan of salted boiling water, cook the green beans until crisp-tender, about 3 minutes. Transfer the beans to the ice bath to cool, then drain.

2 In a medium bowl, combine the yogurt, buttermilk, mustard, lemon juice and tarragon and mix well. Season the dressing with salt.

3 In a large ovenproof skillet, heat the olive oil until shimmering. Season the chicken with salt and pepper, add to the skillet skin side down and cook over moderate heat until golden and crisp, about 8 minutes. Turn the chicken skin side up and roast in the oven for 10 to 12 minutes, until cooked through and an instant-read thermometer inserted into the thickest part registers 160°.

4 Add the butter, thyme and garlic to the skillet and cook over moderate heat for 2 minutes, basting the chicken constantly. Let rest for 5 minutes.

5 Add the green beans to the buttermilk-tarragon dressing and toss to coat. Season with salt and pepper. Serve the chicken with the green beans.

MAKE AHEAD The dressing can be refrigerated for up to 2 days.

▲ **2009** Cooks for the band Jane's Addiction at Lollapalooza; returns the following year as culinary director for the festival, curating the vendor lineup and elevating the offerings.

For this Southern-inspired dish, Elliot gives pork tenderloin incredible flavor with a quick brine in sweet tea and aromatic spices.

PORK TENDERLOIN WITH FRIED OKRA & PICKLED WATERMELON

ACTIVE 30 min **TOTAL** 2 hr **MAKES** 4 servings

½ cup plus 1 tablespoon sugar
½ tablespoon unseasoned rice vinegar
2 jalapeño slices
2 cups diced watermelon
1 cup kosher salt, plus more for seasoning
3 cardamom pods, lightly crushed
6 black peppercorns
6 coriander seeds
1 black tea bag, such as English Breakfast
Two 1-pound pork tenderloins
2 tablespoons olive oil
Canola oil, for frying
¼ cup cornmeal
¼ cup cornstarch
¼ cup all-purpose flour
½ teaspoon Old Bay Seasoning
¼ teaspoon smoked paprika
¼ teaspoon dried ground sumac (see Note)
1 cup buttermilk
12 okra

PAIR WITH Lively, watermelon-scented rosé: 2012 Jean-Paul Brun Rosé d'Folie

1 In a large bowl, mix 1 tablespoon of the sugar with 1 tablespoon of water until the sugar has dissolved. Add the vinegar and jalapeño and let stand for 10 minutes. Remove and discard the jalapeño. Add the watermelon to the bowl, toss to coat and let stand for 1 hour, tossing occasionally. Drain the watermelon and season with salt.

2 Meanwhile, in a large saucepan, combine the 1 cup of salt with the remaining ½ cup of sugar and the cardamom, peppercorns, coriander seeds, tea bag and 2 quarts of water. Bring to a simmer. Strain the brine into a large heatproof bowl and let cool completely. Immerse the pork tenderloins in the brine and let stand at room temperature for 45 minutes. Rinse the pork and pat dry.

3 Preheat the oven to 375°. In a large ovenproof skillet, heat the olive oil. Add the pork and cook on all sides until golden brown, about 5 minutes. Transfer the pork to the oven and roast for about 15 minutes, until an instant-read thermometer inserted in the thickest part of the meat registers 150°. Let the pork rest for 15 minutes.

4 Heat 1 inch of canola oil in a medium, heavy pot until it reaches 350° on a candy thermometer. In a medium bowl, whisk together the cornmeal, cornstarch, flour, Old Bay, smoked paprika, sumac and ½ teaspoon of salt. Pour the buttermilk into a small bowl. Dip the okra in the buttermilk, then dredge in the cornmeal mixture. Fry the okra until tender and golden brown, 2 to 3 minutes. Transfer the fried okra to a paper towel–lined plate.

5 Slice the pork and serve with the pickled watermelon and fried okra.

NOTE Sumac is a fruity, tart berry that grows wild in the Middle East and Italy. Dried ground sumac can be purchased at Middle Eastern markets, specialty food stores or online at *kalustyans.com*.

▲ **2010** Debuts as a judge on the FOX competitive cooking show *MasterChef*.

DANIEL HUMM

BEST NEW CHEF '05

Swiss-born chef Daniel Humm is an idea machine. At Manhattan's Eleven Madison Park, he received the kind of accolades every chef dreams of. But he still felt restless. So he and his business partner and creative collaborator, Will Guidara, decided to take a risk and rethink the whole experience. Today, Eleven Madison is as much about drama as phenomenal food: a carrot tartare ground table-side, a table-top clambake, a liquid-nitrogen cocktail served in the kitchen. At The NoMad (left), Humm also produces showstoppers like a whole chicken for two packed shamelessly with truffles— perhaps the most luxurious roast chicken in America.

1990 Hoping to follow in his father's footsteps, Humm interns at an architectural firm in Zurich.

Humm's terrific summer salad is crisp and lemony, with bits of meaty pancetta and lots of fresh mint. Since the snow peas are raw, it's best to buy super-fresh ones, preferably from a farmers' market.

FRESH SNOW PEA SALAD WITH PANCETTA & PECORINO

TOTAL 35 min   **MAKES** 6 to 8 servings

- 1 pound snow peas—strings removed, pods sliced on the diagonal ¼ inch wide
- ¼ cup plus 1 tablespoon extra-virgin olive oil
- 4 ounces thickly sliced pancetta, cut into ¼-inch dice
- ½ small white onion, finely chopped
- 2 tablespoons fresh lemon juice
- ½ teaspoon lemon oil (see Note)
- Kosher salt and freshly ground black pepper
- ½ cup mint leaves, torn
- 2 ounces Pecorino Sardo cheese

PAIR WITH Lively, light-bodied Sicilian white: 2011 Tami Grillo

1. Soak the snow peas in a medium bowl of ice water for 10 minutes.

2. Meanwhile, in a medium skillet, heat 1 tablespoon of the olive oil. Add the pancetta and cook over moderate heat until lightly browned and the fat has rendered, about 5 minutes. Spoon off all but 1 tablespoon of the fat. Add the onion and cook, stirring occasionally, until softened, about 5 minutes.

3. Drain the snow peas and pat dry. In a medium bowl, whisk the remaining ¼ cup of olive oil with the lemon juice and lemon oil and season with salt and pepper. Add the snow peas, pancetta, onion and half of the mint and season with salt and pepper; toss well. Garnish with the remaining mint, shave the pecorino on top and serve.

NOTE Olive oil pressed or infused with lemon is available at specialty food stores and most supermarkets.

Airy, light and fluffy, Humm's homemade bread is the ultimate focaccia. He tops it with roasted cherry tomatoes and garlic confit, garlic cloves cooked slowly in rosemary-lemon oil until they're sweet and tender.

TOMATO & GARLIC CONFIT FOCACCIA

TOTAL 3 hr plus overnight refrigerating   **MAKES** two 11-by-14-inch focaccia

DOUGH
5 to 5½ cups bread flour
2¼ teaspoons active dry yeast (1 packet)
2 teaspoons kosher salt
3 tablespoons extra-virgin olive oil, plus more for greasing

TOPPINGS
1 pound cherry tomatoes, halved
Kosher salt and freshly ground black pepper
1¼ cups extra-virgin olive oil
1½ cups peeled garlic cloves (7 ounces)
2 tablespoons rosemary leaves
1 tablespoon crushed red pepper
Zest of 1 lemon, removed with a vegetable peeler
Sea salt
Freshly grated Parmigiano-Reggiano cheese
Torn basil leaves

1 **MAKE THE DOUGH** In a standing mixer fitted with the dough hook, combine the flour, yeast and salt with the 3 tablespoons of olive oil and 2½ cups of cold water. Mix at low speed until the flour is evenly moistened. Beat at medium speed until the dough is smooth and glossy, about 3 minutes longer; the dough will be soft and somewhat sticky. Transfer the dough to an oiled baking sheet, cover with a bowl and let rest for 20 minutes.

2 With lightly floured hands, press the dough into an 8-inch square and fold it in thirds. Rotate the baking sheet and fold the dough in thirds again. Cover the dough with the bowl and let rest for 20 minutes. Repeat the folding and resting twice more.

3 Divide the dough in half and place each piece in a lightly oiled bowl. Cover with plastic wrap and refrigerate overnight.

4 **MAKE THE TOPPINGS** Preheat the oven to 300°. On a baking sheet lined with parchment paper, arrange the tomatoes cut side up and season them with kosher salt and black pepper. Roast for about 1 hour, until the tomatoes are slightly dry but soft.

5 Meanwhile, in a small ovenproof saucepan, combine the olive oil, garlic, rosemary, crushed red pepper and lemon zest and bring to a simmer over moderate heat. Cover, transfer to the oven and cook until the garlic is tender and lightly golden, about 35 minutes. Discard the lemon zest; let the garlic cool in the oil.

6 Bring the dough to room temperature. Generously oil 2 baking sheets. Stretch each piece of dough into an 11-by-14-inch rectangle on a baking sheet and let rest for 30 minutes.

7 Increase the oven temperature to 475°. Arrange the tomatoes cut side up on the dough and drizzle with some of the garlic oil. Dot the focaccia with the garlic confit. Bake the focaccia in the upper and lower thirds of the oven until golden and crusty, about 20 minutes, shifting the pans from top to bottom and front to back halfway through baking. Sprinkle with sea salt, cheese and basil, drizzle with some of the garlic oil and serve.

This clever mix of sweet and savory ingredients can be served as a light first course or an elegant dessert. Humm makes the recipe with apricots, but peaches also work well.

ROASTED PEACHES WITH TOMATOES, ALMONDS & HERBS

ACTIVE 1 hr 15 min **TOTAL** 3 hr 15 min **MAKES** 8 servings

2 tablespoons sugar
Kosher salt
8 small peaches or large apricots, halved and pitted
2¾ cups extra-virgin olive oil
2¾ cups canola oil
8 garlic cloves, lightly smashed
4 rosemary sprigs, broken into pieces
4 basil sprigs
2 thyme sprigs
2 bay leaves
Zest of 1 lemon, removed with a vegetable peeler
1 cup blanched almonds
¼ cup white balsamic vinegar
2 pints heirloom cherry tomatoes, halved
2 ounces *ricotta salata,* shaved
Balsamic vinegar, for drizzling
Marjoram and basil leaves, for garnish

PAIR WITH Fragrant, full-bodied white: 2012 Éric Texier Côtes du Rhône Blanc

1 In a large bowl, combine the sugar with ½ tablespoon of salt. Add the peaches and toss to coat, then spread them in a single layer in a 9-by-13-inch baking dish.

2 In a large saucepan, combine 2 cups of the olive oil with 2 cups of the canola oil and the garlic and heat until the oil reaches 140° on a candy thermometer. Add 1 rosemary sprig along with the basil, thyme, bay leaves and lemon zest and let steep off the heat for 1 hour.

3 Preheat the oven to 225°. Bring the infused oil just to a simmer, then strain it over the peaches. Cover the baking dish with foil and roast the peaches until tender but not falling apart, about 45 minutes. Let cool slightly. Using a slotted spoon, transfer the peaches to a plate; reserve the oil.

4 Increase the oven temperature to 300°. In a small bowl, toss the almonds with 2 tablespoons of the reserved peach oil. Spread the almonds on a baking sheet and toast in the oven until golden, about 20 minutes. Let cool, then sprinkle with salt.

5 In a medium bowl, combine the remaining ¾ cup of olive oil with the white balsamic vinegar and season with salt. Add the tomatoes, toss and let stand for 10 minutes.

6 Meanwhile, in a small saucepan, heat the remaining ¾ cup of canola oil until it reaches 350°. Add the remaining 3 rosemary sprigs and fry until darkened and crispy, about 30 seconds. Using a slotted spoon, transfer the rosemary to paper towels and sprinkle with salt.

7 Drain the tomatoes. Arrange the peaches and tomatoes on plates. Scatter the toasted almonds all around and top with the *ricotta salata.* Drizzle each plate with some of the reserved peach oil and balsamic vinegar. Garnish with the fried rosemary sprigs and fresh marjoram and basil and serve right away.

MAKE AHEAD The roasted peaches can be refrigerated in the oil for up to 3 days.

2006 Relocates to New York City to become the chef at Danny Meyer's Eleven Madison Park.

As a child, Humm drank a glass of warm milk with honey before bedtime. At The NoMad, he reimagines the drink as a cold dessert. For drizzling over vanilla ice cream, he likes the visual contrast of a darker buckwheat honey but says it's fine to use any kind of honey in the crumble and brittle.

MILK & HONEY

ACTIVE 30 min **TOTAL** 2 hr **MAKES** 6 servings

HONEY-OAT CRUMBLE

- 5 tablespoons unsalted butter, softened
- 3 tablespoons sugar
- 2 tablespoons honey
- ½ teaspoon pure vanilla extract
- ½ teaspoon kosher salt
- 1 cup plus ½ tablespoon all-purpose flour
- ¼ cup thick-cut rolled oats
- ⅛ teaspoon baking soda

HONEY BRITTLE

- 1 cup sugar
- 4 tablespoons unsalted butter
- 2 tablespoons honey
- 1½ teaspoons kosher salt
- ½ teaspoon baking soda

Vanilla ice cream, for serving
Buckwheat honey, for drizzling

1 MAKE THE HONEY-OAT CRUMBLE Preheat the oven to 300° and line a baking sheet with parchment paper. In a standing mixer fitted with the paddle, beat the butter with the sugar, honey, vanilla and salt until smooth. Add the flour, oats and baking soda and beat at low speed until a stiff batter forms.

2 Using an offset spatula, spread the batter onto the parchment in a rough rectangle ¼ inch thick. Bake in the center of the oven for 15 minutes, until lightly golden. Reduce the oven temperature to 200° and bake until deeply golden and firm, about 40 minutes longer. Let cool completely, then break the crumble into pieces.

3 MEANWHILE, MAKE THE HONEY BRITTLE Line a large baking sheet with parchment paper. In a small saucepan, combine the sugar, butter, honey and salt with ¼ cup of water. Bring to a boil, washing down any crystals from the side of the pan with a moistened pastry brush. Cook over moderately high heat, without stirring, until the syrup reaches 300° on a candy thermometer, about 10 minutes. Remove from the heat. Stir in the baking soda and immediately pour the mixture onto the parchment paper in a thin layer without disturbing the bubbles. Let the honey brittle cool completely, then break into shards.

4 Sprinkle some of the honey brittle into bowls and top with scoops of ice cream. Drizzle with buckwheat honey and garnish with the honey-oat crumble.

MAKE AHEAD The honey-oat crumble and honey brittle can be stored in separate airtight containers at room temperature for up to 1 week.

2011 With general manager Will Guidara, purchases Eleven Madison Park from Danny Meyer's Union Square Hospitality Group.

DAVID CHANG

BEST NEW CHEF '06

When David Chang opened Momofuku Noodle Bar in Manhattan in 2004, it seemed bizarre that a chef who'd worked for a luminary like Daniel Boulud would want to run a ramen joint. Yet with his driving dcsirc to serve the best ramen he could, he invented a new kind of hip-yet-elevated restaurant. Since then, Chang has expanded his NYC empire, earning two Michelin stars at Momofuku Ko; recently, he opened Momofuku outposts in Toronto and Sydney. Meanwhile, at his culinary lab in Manhattan, he continues to explore new ways to create umami, part of the ongoing Momofuku experiment.

1990 Becomes a junior golf champion but suffers burnout and quits competing at 13.

This light and elegant no-cook dish features custardy silken tofu in an ultra-refreshing broth. Here, Chang uses umami-packed shiro dashi, *a bottled Japanese stock, as the savory base for the broth, stirring in Fuji apple juice for just the right amount of sweetness.*

COLD TOFU WITH CHESTNUTS IN APPLE DASHI

TOTAL 20 min　　**MAKES** 4 first-course servings

2　cups Fuji apple juice (see Note)
3　tablespoons *shiro* dashi (see Note)
2　tablespoons soy sauce
½　tablespoon sherry vinegar
½　tablespoon untoasted sesame oil
One 12-ounce package soft silken tofu, drained and sliced
2　cooked chestnuts, thinly sliced
Light green frisée leaves and wasabi oil (see Note), for garnish

PAIR WITH Full-bodied, apple-scented orange wine: 2010 Monastero Suore Cistercensi Coenobium Rusticum

In a small bowl, whisk the apple juice with the *shiro* dashi, soy sauce, sherry vinegar and sesame oil. Arrange the tofu slices in shallow bowls. Top with the chestnuts and frisée. Pour the apple dashi around the tofu. (Reserve any remaining apple dashi for another use.) Drizzle each bowl with a few drops of wasabi oil and serve.

NOTE Fuji apple juice is available at supermarkets and juice bars, or you can make your own. *Shiro* dashi is a stock made with soy sauce, white soy, bonito flakes and seaweed. *Shiro* dashi and wasabi oil are both available at Japanese and Korean markets.

▶ **2000** Answers the phones for no pay at Tom Colicchio's new Craft restaurant in Manhattan; gets the opportunity to prep vegetables and works his way up to line cook.

Chang revamps standard lentil soup with mild miso, which adds depth and complexity. He tops each bowl with crispy fried celery root and a warm sabayon-style sauce that's rich with egg yolks and smoky bacon.

LENTIL MISO SOUP WITH BACON SABAYON

ACTIVE 1 hr   **TOTAL** 2 hr   **MAKES** 8 servings

SOUP

Two 6-inch squares of kombu (dried seaweed; see Note on page 198)
- 1 ounce dried shiitake mushrooms, crumbled
- 1 bay leaf
- 4 thyme sprigs
- 1 teaspoon black peppercorns
- 2 tablespoons grapeseed oil
- 1 small onion, finely chopped
- 1 medium carrot, finely chopped
- 1 medium celery rib, finely chopped
- 1 garlic clove, minced
- 1¼ cups French lentils (about ½ pound), rinsed
- ½ cup *shiro* miso (light yellow)

Salt and freshly ground pepper
- 1 tablespoon unsalted butter
- ¾ cup peeled and cubed (½-inch cubes) celery root

BACON SABAYON

- 4 ounces slab bacon, thinly sliced and cut into fine matchsticks
- 6 large egg yolks
- 1½ teaspoons cider vinegar
- 1½ teaspoons soy sauce

PAIR WITH Juicy, Grenache-based Côtes du Rhône: 2011 Domaine Pelaquie

1 MAKE THE SOUP In a large pot, combine the kombu with 10 cups of water and bring just to a simmer. Cover and let stand off the heat for 10 minutes. Discard the kombu. Add the shiitake to the pot along with the bay leaf, thyme and peppercorns and bring to a boil. Cover and let stand off the heat for 10 minutes. Strain the dashi (broth) into a heatproof bowl; you should have 8 cups. Discard the solids and wipe out the pot.

2 In the same pot, heat 1 tablespoon of the oil. Add the onion, carrot, celery and garlic and cook over low heat until softened, about 8 minutes. Add the lentils and the 8 cups of dashi and bring to a boil. Cover partially and simmer over moderately low heat until the lentils are tender, about 1 hour.

3 Working in batches, puree the soup in a blender or food processor with the miso until smooth. Return the soup to the pot; add a few tablespoons of water if it is very thick. Season with salt and pepper and keep warm.

4 In a medium skillet, melt the butter in the remaining 1 tablespoon of grapeseed oil. Add the celery root, season with salt and pepper and cook over moderate heat, stirring occasionally, until crisp-tender and lightly browned, about 7 minutes. Transfer to a plate and keep warm.

5 MAKE THE BACON SABAYON In the same skillet, cook the bacon over moderate heat until browned and crispy, 5 to 6 minutes. Strain the fat into a heatproof bowl and reserve 3 tablespoons. Drain the bacon on paper towels.

6 In a large heatproof bowl, whisk the egg yolks with 1½ teaspoons of warm water. Set the bowl over a pan of simmering water (do not let the bowl touch the water) and whisk the eggs constantly until thick and ribbony, about 5 minutes. Whisk the 3 tablespoons of reserved bacon fat into the sabayon in a thin stream and cook until thick and billowy, about 1 minute. Gradually whisk in the cider vinegar and soy sauce and whisk for about 1 minute longer.

7 Serve the soup in shallow bowls and garnish with the celery root, sabayon and crispy bacon.

MAKE AHEAD The soup can be prepared through Step 3 and refrigerated for up to 3 days. Thin with water if necessary.

This rustic pasta is easy to make from scratch in a standing mixer. Chang tosses it in an equally simple butter glaze along with goat cheese, fresh herbs and spicy quick-pickled tomatoes.

HAND-TORN PASTA WITH PICKLED TOMATOES & HERBS

ACTIVE 1 hr 15 min   **TOTAL** 2 hr 15 min   **MAKES** 6 servings

PICKLED TOMATOES
- ¾ cup unseasoned rice vinegar
- 1 tablespoon tamari
- 1½ teaspoons Asian fish sauce
- ¼ cup thinly sliced peeled fresh ginger
- 5 Thai bird chiles
- 1 tablespoon sugar
- 1 pint grape tomatoes, pricked with a skewer

PASTA
- 3 large eggs plus 3 large egg yolks
- 3 tablespoons grapeseed oil
- 2 cups all-purpose flour, plus more for rolling

Kosher salt
- 2 tablespoons finely shredded peeled fresh ginger
- ⅓ cup thinly sliced spring onions or scallion whites
- 5 tablespoons unsalted butter
- 1 long fresh hot red chile, seeded and thinly sliced
- ¼ cup shredded basil
- ¼ cup shredded mint
- 4 ounces fresh goat cheese, crumbled

PAIR WITH Floral, full-bodied Spanish white: 2012 Finca Os Cobatos Godello

1 MAKE THE PICKLED TOMATOES In a medium saucepan, combine the rice vinegar, tamari, fish sauce, ginger, chiles, sugar and ½ cup of water and bring to a simmer over moderate heat. Let cool slightly, then add the tomatoes. Let stand at room temperature for 2 hours. Drain the tomatoes; discard the ginger and chiles.

2 MEANWHILE, MAKE THE PASTA In a standing mixer fitted with the paddle, combine the eggs, egg yolks and 2 tablespoons of the oil. Add the 2 cups of flour and 1½ teaspoons of salt and mix until the dough comes together. Knead the dough on an unfloured surface for 30 seconds, then wrap in plastic and let stand at room temperature for 1 hour.

3 Cut the dough into 2 pieces. Working with 1 piece at a time and keeping the other covered, roll the dough through successively narrower settings on a pasta machine until the pasta is very thin. Dust with flour and let stand on a work surface, turning the pasta once or twice, until slightly dry, about 30 minutes. Tear the pasta into 2-inch pieces and toss with flour.

4 Bring a large pot of generously salted water to a boil. Add the pasta and cook until al dente, about 3 minutes. Drain, reserving ½ cup of the cooking water.

5 In a large skillet, heat the remaining 1 tablespoon of grapeseed oil. Add the ginger and onions and cook over moderate heat until softened, about 2 minutes. Add the ½ cup of pasta cooking water and bring to a boil. Add the butter and simmer over low heat, shaking the pan, until the sauce is creamy. Add the pasta, red chile slices, basil and mint and toss until evenly coated. Add the goat cheese and pickled tomatoes and serve right away.

MAKE AHEAD The torn pasta can be frozen on a baking sheet until firm, then transferred to a sturdy plastic bag and frozen for 1 month.

One of Chang's favorite ingredients in his arsenal of flavor boosters is kombu, a dried kelp that's typically simmered for stocks and soups. He pulverizes the kombu to a powder and blends it with softened butter to baste striped bass fillets.

ROAST BASS WITH KOMBU BUTTER, ICEBERG LETTUCE & ASPARAGUS

TOTAL 45 min   **MAKES** 6 servings

One 4-inch square of kombu (dried seaweed; see Note)
1 stick unsalted butter, softened
½ large head of iceberg lettuce, cut into 6 wedges
2 tablespoons canola oil, plus more for rubbing
Sea salt and freshly ground pepper
¾ pound asparagus
2 teaspoons sherry vinegar
Six 4-ounce striped bass fillets with skin, skin scored lightly in 3 slashes
Crumbled seasoned nori sheets, for garnish
Lemon wedges, for serving

PAIR WITH Lemony, medium-bodied Austrian white: 2012 Nigl Kremser Freiheit Grüner Veltliner

1 Microwave the kombu in 10-second bursts at medium power for 30 seconds; be careful not to let it scorch. Let cool completely until crisp. Break the kombu into pieces and grind to a powder in a spice grinder. In a small bowl, combine the softened butter with the kombu powder.

2 Preheat the oven to 375°. Heat a large skillet. Rub the iceberg wedges lightly with oil and season with salt and pepper. Add them to the skillet and cook over moderately high heat, turning once, until lightly charred, about 2 minutes. Transfer to a platter, cover loosely with foil and keep warm.

3 In the same skillet, melt 2 tablespoons of the kombu butter. Add the asparagus and cook over moderately high heat, turning occasionally, until tender and browned in spots, about 4 minutes. Add the vinegar and toss; keep warm.

4 In an ovenproof nonstick or cast-iron skillet, heat the 2 tablespoons of oil until shimmering. Season the fish fillets with salt and pepper and add them to the skillet, skin side down. Set another skillet on top of the fish and cook over moderately high heat for 1 minute to flatten and sear the skin. Remove the top skillet and cook the fish until browned on the bottom, about 2 minutes longer. Transfer the skillet to the oven and roast the fish until cooked through, about 5 minutes.

5 Return the skillet to moderate heat and add 3 tablespoons of the kombu butter. Spoon the melted butter all over the fish. Arrange the fish, lettuce and asparagus on plates. Spoon the remaining 3 tablespoons of kombu butter on top. Garnish with nori and sprinkle with sea salt. Serve at once, with lemon wedges.

NOTE Kombu is available at Japanese markets, health-food stores and some supermarkets as well as online at *edenfoods.com.*

MAKE AHEAD The kombu butter can be refrigerated for up to 3 days.

GABRIEL RUCKER

BEST NEW CHEF '07

07

If any city loves an indie sensibility, Portland, Oregon, does. And one chef who helped shape the city's proud indie identity is Gabriel Rucker of Le Pigeon. Brains, tongue, lips, feet—Rucker uses all kinds of animal parts in French-American dishes, such as squab-head soup. Even salads like his escarole hearts with pickled squash and sage dressing (page 202) have that I'll-do-what-I-want attitude. It has made Le Pigeon one of Portland's toughest reservations, and has also spawned a cookbook, *Le Pigeon*. A bistro offshoot, Little Bird, is more traditional; but with dishes like snail tortellini, it still has the Rucker vibe.

1998 Rucker gets his professional start rolling bagels in a Napa bakery; he typically comes straight to work after staying out all night at clubs and raves.

Quick-pickling raw butternut squash in cider vinegar, sugar and salt makes it tangy and crunchy. Rucker tosses the pickled squash with pleasantly bitter greens and a creamy, garlicky sage dressing.

ESCAROLE WITH PICKLED BUTTERNUT SQUASH

ACTIVE 45 min   **MAKES** 8 servings

1 cup plus 2 tablespoons apple cider vinegar

2 tablespoons sugar

Kosher salt

3 ounces butternut squash, peeled and cut into ¼-inch dice (½ cup)

1 large egg yolk or 3 tablespoons mayonnaise

1 tablespoon freshly grated Parmigiano-Reggiano cheese

6 large sage leaves

1 garlic clove

1 teaspoon fresh lemon juice

⅓ cup canola oil

Freshly ground pepper

1 head of escarole (12 ounces), inner yellow and light green leaves only, torn into bite-size pieces

1 In a medium saucepan, combine 1 cup of the apple cider vinegar with the sugar, 1 tablespoon of salt and ¼ cup of water and bring to a boil. Add the diced squash and let cool to room temperature. Drain the pickled squash.

2 Meanwhile, in a food processor, combine the egg yolk with the cheese, sage, garlic, lemon juice and the remaining 2 tablespoons of vinegar. With the machine on, drizzle in the oil until emulsified. Season the dressing with salt and pepper.

3 In a large bowl, toss the escarole with the dressing and season with salt. Arrange the greens on plates, top with the pickled squash and serve.

MAKE AHEAD The drained pickled squash and the dressing can be refrigerated for up to 2 days.

Rucker conceived of this inventive salmon dish after sniffing a bag of porcini powder. "The aroma reminded me of cinnamon," he says. "So I opened a jar of cinnamon and smelled the two together. Voilà! It worked."

SALMON POACHED IN CINNAMON BUTTER WITH CEDAR-PLANKED PORCINI

ACTIVE 30 min   **TOTAL** 1 hr 30 min plus 1 hr soaking   **MAKES** 4 servings

MUSHROOMS

1   cedar grilling plank, soaked in water to cover for 1 hour and drained

Canola oil, for greasing the plank

1   garlic clove, minced
1   shallot, minced
1   teaspoon chopped thyme
1   tablespoon extra-virgin olive oil
1   tablespoon aged balsamic vinegar
½   teaspoon kosher salt
½   pound porcini or king trumpet mushrooms, cut into bite-size pieces

SALMON

1   pound unsalted butter
2   teaspoons cinnamon

Four 6-ounce skinless salmon fillets

Kosher salt

Sea salt

Lemon wedges, for serving

PAIR WITH Spicy, cranberry-scented Oregon Pinot Noir: 2011 The Eyrie Vineyards

1 **PREPARE THE MUSHROOMS** Preheat the oven to 375°. Rub the cedar plank with canola oil, transfer it to a baking sheet and heat in the oven for 30 minutes.

2 Meanwhile, in a medium bowl, combine the garlic, shallot, thyme, olive oil, vinegar and salt. Add the mushrooms and toss to coat. Let marinate at room temperature for 30 minutes.

3 Spread out the mushrooms on the cedar plank and roast them until they are tender, about 20 minutes.

4 **MEANWHILE, PREPARE THE SALMON** In a small, deep skillet, combine the butter and cinnamon. Attach a candy thermometer to the side of the skillet. Melt the butter over low heat until it registers 125°. Season the salmon fillets with kosher salt and add them to the skillet; they should be completely submerged in butter. Poach the salmon, turning the fillets halfway, until just cooked through, about 20 minutes; you may have to move the skillet off and on the heat to keep the temperature between 125° and 130°.

5 Transfer the salmon to a paper towel–lined plate and drain briefly. Season with sea salt. Serve with the mushrooms and lemon wedges.

Rucker gives Thai lemongrass chicken soup a French makeover with white wine, sweet potatoes and heavy cream. The result is a rich, warming stew of super-tender chicken thighs.

CHICKEN STEW WITH SHIITAKE & LEMONGRASS

ACTIVE 45 min   **TOTAL** 1 hr 45 min   **MAKES** 4 servings

One 12-ounce sweet potato, peeled and cut into ½-inch dice
¼ cup extra-virgin olive oil
½ teaspoon paprika
¼ teaspoon piment d'Espelette
Kosher salt
4 bone-in chicken thighs with skin
2 tablespoons canola oil
4 large shiitake mushrooms, stems discarded and caps halved
10 garlic cloves, halved
4 large shallots (6 ounces), cut into thick rings
1 tablespoon minced fresh lemongrass (inner bulb only)
1 cup dry white wine
3 cups low-sodium chicken broth
½ cup heavy cream
1 teaspoon Asian fish sauce
1 teaspoon Sriracha

PAIR WITH Zesty, focused Chablis: 2011 Gilbert Picq

1 Preheat the oven to 400°. On a rimmed baking sheet, toss the diced sweet potato with the olive oil, paprika and piment d'Espelette. Season with salt. Roast the sweet potato for about 10 minutes, stirring halfway, until golden and tender. Reduce the oven temperature to 350°.

2 Meanwhile, season the chicken thighs with salt. In a medium enameled cast-iron casserole, heat the canola oil. Add the chicken and cook over moderately high heat until browned all over, about 7 minutes. Transfer the chicken to a plate. Add the mushrooms, garlic, shallots and lemongrass to the casserole and cook, stirring, for 2 minutes. Add the white wine and bring to a boil. Simmer for 2 minutes, stirring to dissolve any browned bits on the bottom of the casserole. Add the chicken broth, heavy cream, fish sauce and Sriracha.

3 Return the chicken thighs to the casserole and bring to a boil. Cover and braise the chicken in the oven for about 1 hour, until very tender.

4 Spoon the roasted sweet potato into bowls. Top with the chicken thighs and mushroom sauce and serve.

MAKE AHEAD The chicken stew can be refrigerated for up to 2 days.

▲ **2006** Takes over as head chef at a failing French bistro; the owners give him two months to break even. He does, renaming the place Le Pigeon.

Although Rucker has had no formal training in French kitchens, his version of the classic blanquette de veau *is delicious. Instead of using flour for thickening, he whisks in extra egg yolks, creating an ultra-rich, velvety cream sauce.*

VEAL BLANQUETTE

ACTIVE 30 min   **TOTAL** 3 hr   **MAKES** 4 servings

2 celery ribs, halved
1 yellow onion, halved
1 head of garlic, halved crosswise
1 leek, white and light green parts only, halved lengthwise
4 thyme sprigs
3 bay leaves
1 tablespoon white peppercorns
Kosher salt
2 pounds veal stew meat, cut into 2-inch cubes
2 cups dry white wine
1 cup curly egg noodles
1 cup frozen white pearl onions (4 ounces), thawed
2 cups small white button mushrooms (6 ounces)
4 large egg yolks
½ cup heavy cream
Freshly ground black pepper

PAIR WITH Creamy, baking spice–scented Pinot Blanc: 2011 Domaine Paul Blanck

1 In a large pot, combine the celery, yellow onion, garlic, leek, thyme, bay leaves, peppercorns and 1 tablespoon of salt. Add the veal, wine and 4 cups of water and bring to a boil. Cover partially and simmer over moderately low heat, skimming occasionally, until the veal is tender, about 2 hours. Using a slotted spoon, transfer the veal to a medium bowl. Strain the cooking liquid into a large heatproof measuring cup; if you don't have at least 3 cups, add water to make 3 cups. Discard the solids; wipe out the pot. Return the liquid to the pot.

2 Meanwhile, cook the egg noodles in a medium pot of boiling water until al dente, 7 to 9 minutes. Drain the noodles, then run them under cold water to cool; drain again.

3 Bring the veal cooking liquid to a boil. Add the pearl onions and button mushrooms and simmer over moderate heat until the mushrooms are tender, about 10 minutes. Add the veal and cook until the liquid has reduced to about 2 cups, about 10 minutes longer.

4 In a small bowl, whisk the egg yolks and cream until well blended. Gradually whisk the egg mixture into the stew and simmer gently until thickened, about 2 minutes. Stir in the noodles and season with salt and pepper. Serve hot.

MAKE AHEAD The veal stew can be refrigerated for up to 2 days. Rewarm gently before adding the noodles.

ETHAN STOWELL

BEST NEW CHEF '08

Seattle chef Ethan Stowell has declared, "I want to be more Italian than anyone else in town." He has achieved this with no fewer than six exceptional Italian restaurants. Stowell owes his success to a willingness to rethink not just the food at each of his places but also the entire dining experience, from communal and loud (Tavolàta) to intimate and den-like (How to Cook a Wolf). Born into a family of ballet professionals, he poses at left with Lindsi Dec and Kylee Kitchens of the Pacific Northwest Ballet.

08

1974 Born in Frankfurt, Germany, to professional ballet dancers; grows up with a Eurocentric focus on home-cooked meals using fresh produce.

Stowell's fresh artichoke salad gets intense flavor from mint and buttery, tender Taggiasca olives. He uses olives packed in their own oil from the Italian importer Ritrovo (ritrovo.com) but says you can make the salad with your favorite olives.

ARTICHOKE & TAGGIASCA OLIVE SALAD WITH PARMIGIANO-REGGIANO

TOTAL 45 min   **MAKES** 4 servings

2   lemons, halved
4   large artichokes
    (about 4 pounds)
1   cup pitted Taggiasca or
    Niçoise olives
¼   cup mint leaves
¼   cup flat-leaf parsley leaves
⅓   cup extra-virgin olive oil
¼   cup fresh lemon juice
Kosher salt and freshly
    ground pepper
One 4-ounce wedge of Parmigiano-
    Reggiano cheese

1 Fill a large bowl with water and squeeze in the juice from the lemon halves. Work with 1 artichoke at a time: Trim the stem, then, using a serrated knife, cut off the top third of the artichoke. Pull off all of the tough outer leaves until only the tender, pale leaves remain. Quarter the artichoke lengthwise and scrape out the furry choke. Add the artichoke quarters to the lemon water and cover with a plate to keep them submerged. Repeat with the remaining 3 artichokes.

2 Fill another large bowl with ice water. Cook the artichokes in a large saucepan of salted boiling water until they are tender in the center, 7 to 8 minutes. Transfer the artichokes to the ice bath to cool. Drain and pat the artichokes dry; wipe out the bowl.

3 In the bowl, combine the artichokes with the olives, mint, parsley, olive oil and lemon juice and season with salt and pepper. Toss to coat. Transfer to a platter. Using a vegetable peeler, shave the cheese over the salad and serve.

▲ **1978** At the age of four, moves with his family to Seattle; learns ballet from his parents but eventually realizes that he'd be a terrible dancer.

This lemony chickpea salad is one of the most popular first-course antipasti at Stowell's Tavolàta. The golden raisins plumped in white wine are sweet and tender.

CHICKPEA SALAD WITH CELERY, GOLDEN RAISINS & LEMON

ACTIVE 15 min **TOTAL** 2 hr 15 min plus overnight soaking **MAKES** 4 servings

1 cup dried chickpeas (about 5 ounces), soaked overnight and drained (see Note)
½ cup golden raisins
½ cup dry white wine
1½ cups thinly sliced celery, plus 1 cup celery leaves
⅓ cup extra-virgin olive oil
¼ cup fresh lemon juice
Kosher salt and freshly ground pepper
½ cup flat-leaf parsley leaves

1 In a large saucepan, cover the chickpeas with 4 inches of water. Bring to a boil and simmer over moderate heat, stirring occasionally, until the chickpeas are tender, about 2 hours; drain the chickpeas.

2 Meanwhile, in a small saucepan, combine the raisins and wine and bring to a boil. Remove from the heat, cover and let stand for 30 minutes. Transfer the raisins and wine to a small bowl and refrigerate until chilled, then drain the raisins.

3 Fill a bowl with ice water. In a medium saucepan of salted boiling water, blanch the sliced celery for 30 seconds, then transfer to the ice bath to stop the cooking. Drain and pat dry.

4 In a medium bowl, whisk the olive oil and lemon juice; season with salt and pepper. Add the raisins, celery, celery leaves, parsley and chickpeas. Toss to coat and season with salt and pepper. Transfer the salad to a platter and serve.

SERVE WITH Crusty bread.

NOTE For a shortcut, you can use two 14-ounce cans of chickpeas, rinsed and drained, instead of dried chickpeas; add them in Step 4.

▶ **1995** Gets his first cooking job at The Ruins, a private dining club in Seattle specializing in themed catering events.

"This is my twist on spaghetti aglio e olio [spaghetti with garlic and oil], which I personally find boring," Stowell says. *He shakes up the classic pasta dish with plenty of anchovies and crushed red pepper and a scattering of garlicky bread crumbs.*

SPAGHETTI WITH GARLIC, HOT PEPPER & ANCHOVIES

TOTAL 45 min   **MAKES** 4 servings

Three 1-inch-thick slices of white bread, crusts removed and bread cubed

½ cup plus 2 tablespoons extra-virgin olive oil

4 garlic cloves—1 lightly crushed, 3 thinly sliced

Kosher salt

1 pound spaghetti

12 oil-packed anchovy fillets, drained and chopped

1 teaspoon crushed red pepper, plus more to taste

¼ cup chopped parsley

Freshly ground black pepper

PAIR WITH Citrusy New Zealand Sauvignon Blanc: 2012 Babich Marlborough

1 In a food processor, pulse the bread until crumbs form; you should get about ⅓ cup. In a small skillet, heat 2 tablespoons of the olive oil. Add the crushed garlic and cook over moderately low heat until the oil is infused with garlic flavor, about 10 minutes. Add the bread crumbs and cook, stirring occasionally, until golden and crisp, 7 to 8 minutes. Season the bread crumbs with salt.

2 Cook the spaghetti in a large pot of salted boiling water until almost al dente (you will cook it more later). Drain the spaghetti, reserving 1 cup of the cooking water.

3 Meanwhile, in a large skillet, heat the remaining ½ cup of olive oil. Add the anchovies and the sliced garlic and cook over moderately low heat, stirring occasionally, until the anchovies have dissolved and the garlic has softened, about 5 minutes. Stir in the crushed red pepper.

4 Add the pasta, ½ cup of the pasta cooking water and the parsley to the skillet and toss until the pasta is well coated in the sauce (add more pasta water if it seems dry). Season with salt and black pepper. Serve the pasta in bowls, sprinkled with the bread crumbs.

Instead of lean pork tenderloin, Stowell likes to use the fattier chuck loin, the last six inches of the cut where the shoulder wraps around the loin. "It's marbled and almost like pork rib eye," he says. Marinating the pork overnight allows the garlic and rosemary flavor to permeate the meat.

GARLIC & ROSEMARY ROAST PORK LOIN

ACTIVE 20 min   **TOTAL** 1 hr 45 min plus overnight marinating   **MAKES** 4 servings

¼ cup plus 2 tablespoons extra-virgin olive oil
8 large garlic cloves, chopped
Leaves from 1 bunch of rosemary, coarsely chopped (½ cup)
2 teaspoons kosher salt
½ teaspoon freshly ground pepper
2 pounds pork loin

PAIR WITH Herb-scented Washington state red blend: 2010 Waters Interlude

1 In a small bowl, stir ¼ cup of the olive oil with the garlic, rosemary, salt and pepper. Rub the mixture all over the pork. Transfer the pork and marinade to a large, resealable plastic bag and refrigerate overnight.

2 Preheat the oven to 400°. Let the pork stand at room temperature for 30 minutes. Brush off as much of the marinade as possible. In a large ovenproof skillet, heat the remaining 2 tablespoons of olive oil until shimmering. Add the pork to the skillet and cook over moderately high heat until browned all over, about 5 minutes. Transfer the pork to the oven and roast for 40 to 45 minutes, until golden and a thermometer inserted in the thickest part of the meat registers 135°. Transfer the pork roast to a work surface or carving board and let rest for 15 minutes before thinly slicing and serving.

SERVE WITH Roasted potatoes.

LINTON HOPKINS

BEST NEW CHEF '09

Atlanta chef Linton Hopkins (at home with his family, left) is the ultimate Slow Food chef—albeit one who cooks heritage-breed pork with an immersion circulator. So committed is he to Southern tradition and local growers that he helped found the Peachtree Road Farmers Market down the road from his flagship, Restaurant Eugene. His Slow Food principles are very much in evidence at his H&F Bread bakery, H&F Bottle Shop and Holeman & Finch Public House gastropub. The last is famous for its burger, freshly ground from locally sourced beef and available to just 24 customers a night—and now also to Braves fans at Turner Field, thanks to a brand-new concession stand.

This recipe employs a technique Hopkins often uses when cooking chicken for his family: He gently poaches an entire chicken in an herbed stock, then serves just the moist breast for dinner. You can use any combination of fresh herbs, but tarragon is especially fragrant in the broth.

SLICED POACHED CHICKEN WITH BABY TURNIPS & MUSHROOMS

ACTIVE 30 min   **TOTAL** 2 hr 45 min   **MAKES** 4 servings

One 3-pound chicken
½ pound beef eye of round
1 onion, quartered
1 celery rib, halved
12 black peppercorns
Handful of mixed herbs—such as
    thyme, tarragon, parsley, chervil
    and chives—plus chopped chives
    and tarragon leaves for garnish
2 bay leaves
Kosher salt
2 tablespoons unsalted butter
12 baby turnips, halved lengthwise
1 leek, white and light green parts
    only, thinly sliced (1 cup)
12 small button mushrooms
Freshly ground pepper
Crusty bread, for serving

PAIR WITH Full-bodied, unoaked California Chardonnay: 2011 Joel Gott

1 Cut the legs and wings off the chicken. Using kitchen shears, remove the back and cut it into 3 pieces.

2 In a large pot, combine the chicken legs, wings and back with the beef, onion, celery, peppercorns, mixed herbs, 1 bay leaf and 1 tablespoon of salt. Lay the chicken breast on top of the herbs. Fill the pot with enough cold water to cover the breast by 1 inch. Bring to a simmer, skimming occasionally. Simmer gently until the breast is cooked through, about 20 minutes. Transfer the chicken breast to a plate and cover loosely with plastic wrap.

3 Continue to simmer the broth, skimming occasionally, until reduced to 8 cups, 1½ to 2 hours. Strain the broth into a medium pot and keep warm; discard the solids.

4 Meanwhile, in a large skillet, melt the butter until it foams. Add the turnips cut side down in a single layer and season with salt. Add the remaining bay leaf and enough water to reach halfway up the sides of the turnips. Bring to a simmer. Cover and cook over moderate heat until the turnips are just tender, about 10 minutes. Add the sliced leek and mushrooms, cover and cook until softened, about 10 minutes. Season with salt and pepper. Discard the bay leaf.

5 Mound the turnips and mushrooms in bowls. Thinly slice the chicken breast and place on top of the vegetables. Pour the broth into the bowls, garnish with the chopped chives and tarragon leaves and serve with crusty bread.

MAKE AHEAD The chicken broth and the poached chicken breast can be refrigerated for up to 3 days.

▶ **1993** Moves to New Orleans to begin a culinary externship for the legendary Brennan family at Mr. B's Bistro.

For this riff on his popular mussels dish served at Holeman & Finch, Hopkins swaps in local Sapelo Island clams. Smoky bacon and bourbon give the dish a Southern twist, while jalapeños add a good amount of heat.

PAN-ROASTED CLAMS WITH BACON, BOURBON & JALAPEÑO

TOTAL 45 min   **MAKES** 4 first-course servings

One 3-ounce slab of smoked bacon, cut into ½-inch dice (½ cup)
¼ cup minced shallots
2 tablespoons minced garlic
2 dozen littleneck clams— scrubbed, soaked in cold water for 15 minutes and drained
¼ cup bourbon
¼ cup bottled clam juice
¼ cup heavy cream
2 jalapeños, thinly sliced into rounds
2 tablespoons minced flat-leaf parsley
2 tablespoons unsalted butter
Crusty bread, for serving

PAIR WITH Vibrant, slightly oaky white: 2011 Belondrade y Lurton Rueda Superior

1 In a large, deep skillet, cook the diced bacon over moderately low heat, stirring occasionally, until the fat has rendered and the bacon has browned, about 10 minutes. With a slotted spoon, transfer the bacon to a plate.

2 Add the shallots and garlic to the skillet and cook over moderately low heat, stirring occasionally, until softened, about 3 minutes. Stir in the clams and bourbon and simmer over moderate heat until the bourbon has almost evaporated. Add the clam juice, cover and cook until the clams open, 5 to 7 minutes. Discard any unopened clams.

3 Transfer the clams to shallow bowls. Add the heavy cream, jalapeños, parsley and bacon to the skillet and simmer for 2 minutes. Swirl in the butter. Pour the sauce over the clams and serve with crusty bread.

After seeing Bobby Flay slather corn on the cob with lime butter before grilling on a cooking show, Hopkins came up with this skillet variation using kernels. To reflect the Central American influence on Southern cuisine, Hopkins adds sweet-hot Padrón peppers, but you can substitute jalapeños.

SKILLET CORN & PEPPERS WITH CILANTRO-LIME MAYO

TOTAL 45 min **MAKES** 4 servings

2 ears of corn—shucked, kernels cut off (2 cups) and cobs reserved
½ cup mayonnaise
½ cup packed cilantro leaves
½ teaspoon finely grated lime zest
1 tablespoon fresh lime juice
Kosher salt
2 tablespoons vegetable oil
12 Padrón peppers or 4 jalapeños
1 tablespoon unsalted butter
Freshly ground pepper

1 In a medium saucepan, simmer the corn cobs in 1 cup of water until the broth has reduced to ¼ cup, about 10 minutes. Strain the broth; discard the cobs.

2 Meanwhile, in a blender, combine the mayonnaise with the cilantro, lime zest and lime juice and puree until smooth. Season with salt.

3 In a cast-iron skillet, heat the oil until smoking. Add the corn kernels and peppers and season with salt. Cover and cook over moderately high heat until the corn starts to pop, 2 to 3 minutes. Stir the corn, cover and cook until the corn is lightly charred, about 2 minutes longer. Add the corn broth and simmer until nearly evaporated, then stir in the butter. Season the corn and peppers with salt and pepper.

4 Transfer the corn and peppers to a bowl, drizzle with some of the cilantro-lime mayonnaise and serve.

▶ **2004** Opens Restaurant Eugene (named for his grandfather) with his wife as sommelier and operations manager; four years later, they open the epic Southern gastropub Holeman & Finch Public House.

"This dish is all about my home state," Hopkins says. *The grouper represents the coast, while the creamy butter beans, tomato and dill exemplify the seasonal bounty. "It's Georgia on a plate."*

PAN-ROASTED GROUPER WITH TOMATO & BUTTER BEAN SALAD

ACTIVE 1 hr   **TOTAL** 2 hr   **MAKES** 4 servings

VINAIGRETTE
- 2 heads of garlic
- ⅓ cup plus 2 tablespoons extra-virgin olive oil
- Kosher salt and freshly ground pepper
- 3 tablespoons sherry vinegar
- 2 teaspoons Dijon mustard
- 1 teaspoon sorghum syrup (see Note) or molasses

SALAD
- ¼ cup extra-virgin olive oil
- 2 tablespoons apple cider vinegar
- 1 tablespoon minced dill
- 2 teaspoons finely grated lemon zest
- 2 tablespoons fresh lemon juice
- Two 14-ounce cans butter beans, drained and rinsed
- 12 ounces cherry tomatoes, halved (2 cups)
- ½ cucumber—peeled, seeded and minced (½ cup)
- 1 large shallot, minced (¼ cup)
- Kosher salt and freshly ground pepper

GROUPER
- 1 tablespoon canola oil
- Four 5-ounce black or red grouper fillets with skin
- Kosher salt
- 2 tablespoons unsalted butter
- 2 thyme sprigs
- ½ lemon

PAIR WITH Lively, Meyer lemon–scented Sonoma Sauvignon Blanc: 2011 Matanzas Creek

1 MAKE THE VINAIGRETTE Preheat the oven to 300°. In a foil-lined cake pan, drizzle the garlic with 2 tablespoons of the olive oil and season with salt and pepper. Roast for about 1½ hours, until soft and caramelized. Let cool.

2 Halve the heads of garlic crosswise. Squeeze out the cloves; discard the skins. In a blender, combine the roasted garlic cloves with the sherry vinegar, mustard and sorghum syrup and puree. With the machine on, drizzle in the remaining ⅓ cup of olive oil until incorporated. Season the roasted garlic vinaigrette with salt and pepper.

3 MAKE THE SALAD In a medium bowl, whisk the olive oil with the apple cider vinegar, dill, lemon zest and lemon juice. Stir in the butter beans, cherry tomatoes, cucumber and shallot. Season the salad with salt and pepper.

4 PREPARE THE GROUPER In a large nonstick skillet, heat the canola oil until shimmering. Season the fish fillets with salt, add to the skillet skin side down and cook over moderate heat until the skin is golden and the fish is cooked halfway through, 5 to 7 minutes. Turn the fillets over and add the butter and thyme sprigs to the skillet. Cook until the grouper is white throughout, basting occasionally with the butter, 5 to 7 minutes longer. Squeeze the lemon over the fish. Discard the thyme sprigs.

5 Spoon the tomato and butter bean salad onto plates. Set the fish on top, drizzle with some of the vinaigrette and serve.

NOTE Sorghum syrup, sometimes referred to as sorghum molasses, is available online at *zingermans.com*.

MAKE AHEAD The vinaigrette can be refrigerated for up to 2 days.

ROY CHOI

BEST NEW CHEF '10

With Los Angeles's Kogi BBQ fleet, Roy Choi showed that it was possible for a chef to prepare remarkable food in a truck. His signature dish, the kimchi taco, also created a new genre of urban cooking that references the many ethnic cuisines of his city—honoring both his Asian heritage and the Mexican grandmas who set up sidewalk grills late at night to feed L.A.'s club kids. With his brick-and-mortar restaurants, Choi continues to come up with intriguing new ideas: chef-y rice bowls (Chego), Asian-fusion picnics (A-Frame), West Indian meets Korean (Sunny Spot). His latest project: working with the owners of New York City's NoMad Hotel for a new property in L.A.'s Koreatown, The Line Hotel.

1978 At eight years old, Choi helps prep food at his family's Korean restaurant in Los Angeles.

"I had an extraordinary Caprese salad at Tra Vigne in Napa Valley and it changed my world," Choi says. For his multiculti take here, tofu and soy sauce stand in for the traditional mozzarella and balsamic. *"It's refreshing without disrupting the romance of the original,"* he says.

TOMATO & TOFU CAPRESE SALAD WITH ASIAN VINAIGRETTE

ACTIVE 30 min   **TOTAL** 2 hr 30 min   **MAKES** 4 servings

6 ounces firm tofu

Three 1-inch-thick slices of white bread, crusts removed and bread cubed

¼ cup plus 2 tablespoons canola oil

¼ cup soy sauce

¼ cup unseasoned rice vinegar

2 tablespoons mirin

1 tablespoon sugar

1 scallion, thinly sliced

1 tablespoon finely grated peeled fresh ginger

1 teaspoon finely grated garlic

Kosher salt and freshly ground pepper

¾ pound tomatoes, cored and sliced

½ cup Thai basil leaves

¼ cup thinly sliced red onion

PAIR WITH Red cherry–scented, full-bodied rosé: 2012 Charles & Charles

1 Set the tofu on a paper towel–lined plate. Cover and chill for at least 2 hours or overnight to drain the excess water. Cut the tofu into ½-inch cubes or rectangles.

2 In a food processor, pulse the bread until coarse crumbs form; you should have about ⅓ cup. In a small skillet, heat 2 tablespoons of the oil. Add the bread crumbs and cook over moderate heat, stirring, until golden, 4 to 5 minutes.

3 In a small bowl, whisk the soy sauce with the vinegar, mirin, sugar, scallion, ginger, garlic and the remaining ¼ cup of oil until emulsified. Season the vinaigrette with salt and pepper.

4 Arrange the tomatoes, tofu, basil and onion Caprese-style on a platter. Drizzle some of the vinaigrette on the salad and top with the bread crumbs. Pass the extra vinaigrette at the table.

MAKE AHEAD The vinaigrette can be refrigerated for up to 2 days.

▲ **1996** While watching *Essence of Emeril* on the Food Network, Choi realizes that he wants to cook professionally; enrolls in the Culinary Institute of America in Hyde Park, New York.

One of Choi's first chef jobs was at an L.A. country club where he made New England clam chowder every Friday. This lighter, Asian-inflected version includes green curry paste, coconut milk and plenty of lime juice.

CURRY-COCONUT CLAM CHOWDER, PAPI-STYLE

TOTAL 45 min **MAKES** 6 servings

- 1 small baking potato, peeled and cut into ½-inch dice
- 4 ounces pancetta or bacon, finely chopped
- 1 tablespoon minced fennel
- 2 garlic cloves, thinly sliced
- 2 tablespoons Thai green curry paste
- ½ cup dry white wine
- One 13-ounce can unsweetened coconut milk
- ¼ cup fresh lime juice
- 2 dozen Manila or littleneck clams
- 3 cups chopped clams with their juices

Kosher salt and freshly ground pepper

Cilantro sprigs, Thai basil and *rau ram* (Vietnamese coriander), for garnish

PAIR WITH Zesty, herb-scented Sauvignon Blanc: 2012 Brander Santa Ynez Valley

1 Cook the potato in a medium saucepan of salted boiling water just until tender, about 5 minutes. Drain.

2 In a large saucepan, cook the pancetta over moderate heat, stirring occasionally, until light golden, 7 to 8 minutes. Add the fennel, garlic and green curry paste and cook, stirring, until fragrant, 1 minute. Add the wine and simmer until reduced by half, about 2 minutes. Add the coconut milk and lime juice and return to a simmer. Add the potato, Manila clams and the chopped clams and their juices. Cover and cook until the Manila clams open, 5 to 7 minutes. Discard any clams that do not open. Season the chowder with salt and pepper. Garnish with cilantro, basil and *rau ram* and serve warm.

▶ **1997** Externs at the legendary Le Bernardin in New York City is ejected from the kitchen six times for cutting fish poorly and burning and oversalting food.

According to Choi, the idea for the wacky yet delicious combination of ingredients in this salad came to him in a dream about Italian grandmothers cooking on Saturn. He balances the flavors with a salsa that gets a double dose of tartness from rice vinegar and purple grape juice.

GRILLED ZUCCHINI WITH BLUEBERRY-HABANERO SALSA

TOTAL 30 min   **MAKES** 8 servings

1 cup blueberries

½ habanero chile, seeded for a milder salsa

¾ cup plus 1 tablespoon basil leaves, preferably opal basil

1 teaspoon finely grated garlic

1 teaspoon finely grated peeled fresh ginger

¼ cup unseasoned rice vinegar

¼ cup purple grape juice

⅓ cup canola oil

3 zucchini (1½ pounds), sliced lengthwise into ⅛-inch-thick strips

2 tablespoons olive oil

Kosher salt and freshly ground pepper

1 In a food processor, combine the blueberries, habanero and ¾ cup of the basil with the garlic, ginger, vinegar and grape juice. With the machine on, add the canola oil in a slow, steady stream until the salsa is blended but still chunky.

2 Light a grill. In a large bowl, toss the zucchini with the olive oil and season with salt and pepper. Grill over moderate heat until lightly charred and tender, 1 to 2 minutes per side.

3 Transfer the zucchini to a platter and garnish with the remaining 1 tablespoon of basil. Serve with the salsa.

MAKE AHEAD The salsa can be refrigerated overnight.

▶ **2008** Rolls out his first Kogi BBQ trucks, serving Korean-style tacos to L.A.; Choi's success sparks a Twitter-dominated food-truck movement across the country.

Choi gives his otherwise classic American cheeseburger an Asian twist by mixing toasted sesame seeds into the mayo and layering minty shiso leaves on top of the lettuce and tomatoes.

DOUBLE CHEESEBURGERS, LOS ANGELES–STYLE

TOTAL 45 min   **MAKES** 4 servings

⅓ cup mayonnaise

1 tablespoon toasted sesame seeds

4 tablespoons unsalted butter, at room temperature

4 brioche hamburger buns, split

2 pounds ground chuck, shaped into eight ¼-inch-thick patties

Kosher salt and freshly ground pepper

2 tablespoons olive oil

8 slices of cheddar cheese

4 butter lettuce leaves

4 shiso or sesame (*perilla*) leaves (see Note)

4 thin slices of tomato

4 thin slices of red onion

Hot sauce, preferably Tapatío, for serving

PAIR WITH Bold, juicy Zinfandel: 2011 Sobon Estate Old Vines

1 In a small bowl, mix the mayonnaise with the sesame seeds.

2 Heat a large nonstick griddle or 2 nonstick skillets over moderate heat. Butter the cut sides of the hamburger buns and toast them on the griddle until golden, 4 to 5 minutes. Transfer to a platter.

3 Season the patties with salt and pepper. Brush the griddle with the olive oil, add the patties and cook over high heat for 2 minutes. Flip the patties and cook for 2 minutes longer, then top each one with a slice of cheddar. Cook just until the cheese has melted, about 1 minute.

4 Stack 2 burgers on each bun. Top with the lettuce, shiso, tomato and onion, then drizzle with hot sauce. Spread the top halves of the buns with the sesame mayo, close the burgers and serve.

NOTE Fresh shiso, a plant in the mint family, is available at Japanese markets. Milder-flavored sesame leaves (sometimes called *perilla*) are available at Korean markets.

CARLO MIRARCHI

BEST NEW CHEF '11

When he opened Roberta's in 2008, Carlo Mirarchi helped pioneer the concept of the chef-driven Brooklyn restaurant. Working out of a ragtag compound that now encompasses a radio station and a farm planted in repurposed shipping containers, the self-taught chef offers customers a choice between fantastic pizzas from an Italian wood-fired oven or dishes worthy of a Michelin-starred tasting menu—or both. At his tasting-menu-only offshoot, Blanca, diners sit in captain's chairs at a 12-seat counter, pick records to play on the turntable, check out the enormous mounted tuna head on the wall and watch Mirarchi and his team prepare a meal of about two dozen courses. It's a one-of-a-kind experience.

1995 At 15 years old, Mirarchi buses tables at a local Italian restaurant on Long Island after school and during the summer.

This salad is a masterful balance of bitter, sweet and salty. Mirarchi uses both the hearts and leaves of puntarelle, a seasonal Italian chicory, topping them with freshly shaved Pecorino Fiore Sardo, a lightly smoked sheep's-milk cheese.

SAUTÉED PUNTARELLE WITH DRIED CHERRIES & PECORINO FIORE SARDO

TOTAL 30 min   **MAKES** 4 servings

2 heads of puntarelle (4 pounds), bottoms trimmed, outer leaves removed and reserved
¼ cup extra-virgin olive oil
⅔ cup dried sour cherries
2 tablespoons sherry vinegar
Kosher salt
One 2-ounce wedge of Pecorino Fiore Sardo cheese

PAIR WITH Juicy, cherry-rich rosé: 2012 Cantele Rosato

1 Chop the puntarelle leaves into 3-inch pieces. Pick off the inner shoots from the hearts and slice them ¼ inch thick.

2 In a large skillet, heat the olive oil. Add the dried cherries and cook over moderately high heat, stirring, for 30 seconds. Add the sliced puntarelle shoots and cook, stirring occasionally, until golden and crisp-tender, 4 to 5 minutes. Add the chopped leaves and vinegar and cook just until the leaves are wilted, 2 minutes. Season with salt.

3 Transfer the puntarelle to plates, shave the pecorino on top and serve.

▶ **2006** Begins cooking at Good World Bar & Grill, a now-defunct Scandinavian restaurant in Manhattan that doubled as a nightclub.

This simple and magical combination of ingredients includes vin cotto (aged vinegar), the superb blue cheese blu di bufala and radicchio (or the milder Castelfranco that Mirarchi prefers). It's a very Italian dish, but Mirarchi gives it a personal imprint by adding fish sauce to the dressing.

WARM RADICCHIO WITH VIN COTTO & BLU DI BUFALA

TOTAL 20 min   **MAKES** 4 servings

2 heads of radicchio or Castelfranco (see Note), trimmed and leaves separated

5 tablespoons extra-virgin olive oil

2 teaspoons Asian fish sauce

2 teaspoons fresh lemon juice, plus 4 lemon wedges for serving

1 teaspoon white balsamic vinegar, plus more to taste

3 ounces *blu di bufala* or Gorgonzola *piccante* cheese, crumbled

Vin cotto or aged balsamic vinegar, for drizzling

PAIR WITH Light-bodied, fruit-forward Dolcetto d'Alba: 2012 Francesco Rinaldi & Figli Roussot

1 In a large bowl, combine the radicchio leaves with 3 tablespoons of the olive oil, the fish sauce and lemon juice; toss to coat the leaves.

2 In a large skillet, heat the remaining 2 tablespoons of olive oil until shimmering. Add the radicchio and cook over moderately high heat, stirring, until it is golden in spots and just wilted, about 2 minutes. Stir in the white balsamic vinegar.

3 Transfer the radicchio to plates and top with the cheese. Drizzle with the *vin cotto* and serve with lemon wedges.

NOTE Castelfranco is a mild member of the radicchio family. It has pale yellow or green leaves with red speckles.

▶ **2007** Partners with his friends Brandon Hoy and Chris Parachini, offering to invest money and serve as chef for a restaurant concept that becomes Roberta's.

Mirarchi often makes this dish with sepia (cuttlefish) and hyssop, an herb with a minty licorice flavor. This version, which calls for easier-to-find squid and fresh mint, is also delicious.

SQUID WITH CITRUS, CHILE & MINT

TOTAL 25 min **MAKES** 4 to 6 first-course servings

¾ pound cleaned squid, bodies cut into 1-inch rings and tentacles cut into 2-inch lengths

Kosher salt and freshly ground pepper

1 pomelo or Oro Blanco grapefruit (see Note), or 4 Cara Cara oranges

2 tablespoons extra-virgin olive oil, plus more for drizzling

Pinch of crushed red pepper

2 tablespoons small mint leaves

PAIR WITH Tangy, zesty Italian white: 2011 Bibi Graetz Casamatta Bianco

1 Place the squid in a medium bowl and season with salt and pepper.

2 Using a sharp knife, carefully peel the pomelo; be sure to remove all of the bitter white pith. Working over a large bowl, cut in between the membranes to release the sections. Chop the sections into ½-inch pieces and return them to the bowl. Squeeze any extra juice from the membranes into the bowl.

3 In a large skillet, heat the 2 tablespoons of olive oil until shimmering. Add the squid and cook over high heat, tossing, until bright white, about 2 minutes. Transfer the squid to the bowl with the pomelo, add the crushed pepper and toss; season with salt. Arrange the squid and pomelo on a platter and top with the mint. Drizzle with olive oil and serve.

NOTE Pomelos are large, thick-rinded yellow or green citrus fruits originally from Asia. They taste similar to grapefruit but are less juicy. Oro Blancos are sweet, thick-rinded, white-fleshed hybrids of pomelos and grapefruit.

▶ **2008** At 27 years old, opens Roberta's in a concrete bunker in industrial Bushwick, Brooklyn.

Sea urchin figured large in Mirarchi's childhood: "Every August, we'd go to Calabria, Italy," he says. "We'd dive for sea urchin, crack them open and eat them right on the beach." Be sure to use the freshest possible sea urchins here.

SEA URCHIN LINGUINE

TOTAL 25 min   **MAKES** 4 first-course servings

4 ounces fresh sea urchin (see Note)
¼ cup extra-virgin olive oil
½ pound linguine
1 cup ramp greens, coarsely chopped, or 3 tablespoons chopped chives (see Note)

PAIR WITH Briny, minerally Muscadet: 2012 Domaine de la Pepière Sèvre et Maine Sur Lie

1 In a blender, puree the sea urchin with 2 tablespoons of the olive oil until smooth.

2 In a pot of heavily salted boiling water, cook the linguine until al dente. Meanwhile, in a deep skillet, heat the remaining 2 tablespoons of olive oil. Add the ramp greens and cook over moderately high heat until they are wilted, about 1 minute.

3 Drain the linguine, reserving 5 tablespoons of the cooking water. Add the linguine, 2 tablespoons of the cooking water and the sea urchin puree to the skillet with the ramp greens and toss over moderate heat for 30 seconds. Off the heat, add the remaining 3 tablespoons of cooking water and toss. Transfer the linguine to bowls and serve.

NOTE Look for *uni* (sea urchin) at Japanese markets. If using chives, toss them with the pasta at the end.

ERIK ANDERSON & JOSH HABIGER

BEST NEW CHEFS '12

Josh Habiger (left) and Erik Anderson trained in some of the best kitchens in the world—Habiger at Alinea in Chicago and The Fat Duck in Bray, England; Anderson at The French Laundry in Napa Valley and Copenhagen's Noma. Yet they've made their home in Nashville, where not many restaurants aim higher than meat-and-three, winning the Best New Chef honor for their cooking at The Catbird Seat. Habiger now focuses on developing new projects for the restaurant's parent company, while Anderson continues to create ambitious yet approachable dishes for The Catbird Seat. Working behind a U-shaped counter that seats 32, he hands plates directly to customers—like maple-and-thyme custard served in an eggshell with bacon crisps and a drizzle of barrel-aged maple syrup.

1983 At the age of 11, Anderson washes dishes at his mother's breakfast/lunch spot in North Aurora, Illinois. **1994** At 15, Habiger washes dishes at a diner in St. Joseph, Minnesota, where his mother was once a waitress.

Anderson created this bread salad using Wonder bread and dill pickles, which always accompany classic Nashville hot chicken. He serves it with The Catbird Seat's spin on hot chicken (page 258) as "a tribute to the city and proof that we don't take ourselves too seriously."

DILL PICKLE PANZANELLA

TOTAL 30 min   **MAKES** 4 to 6 servings

8 to 10 slices of white sandwich
    bread, cut into ½-inch pieces
¼ cup brine from jarred dill pickles
¼ cup canola oil
½ teaspoon sugar
½ cup finely diced dill pickles
½ small red onion,
    very thinly sliced
Kosher salt and freshly ground
    black pepper
 2 cups lightly packed baby arugula
½ cup lightly packed basil leaves,
    torn
½ cup shaved Parmigiano-
    Reggiano cheese

1 Preheat the oven to 350°. Spread the bread on a large rimmed baking sheet and bake for 10 to 12 minutes, until lightly toasted. Let cool completely.

2 In a large bowl, whisk the pickle brine with the canola oil and sugar. Add the toasted bread, pickles and onion and toss well. Season with salt and pepper. Add the arugula, basil and half of the shaved cheese and toss. Transfer the panzanella to a platter and top with the remaining cheese. Serve right away.

SERVE WITH Tea-Brined & Double-Fried Hot Chicken (page 258), hot dogs or sausages.

Habiger's silky soup gets slight heat from red curry paste and sweetness from butternut squash. The bok choy and pickled mushrooms add crunch and tang, but the soup is also delicious on its own.

RED CURRY SQUASH SOUP WITH BOK CHOY & PICKLED MUSHROOMS

ACTIVE 40 min **TOTAL** 1 hr 30 min **MAKES** 8 servings

PICKLED MUSHROOMS
- ½ cup sugar
- ½ cup unseasoned rice vinegar
- ½ cup distilled white vinegar
- 1½ teaspoons kosher salt
- ¾ pound *hon-shimeji* (beech mushrooms), roots trimmed and mushrooms separated
- 3 fresh kaffir lime leaves (see Note)
- 1 thyme sprig

SOUP
- 2 tablespoons vegetable oil
- 1 large onion, thinly sliced
- 8 garlic cloves, finely chopped
- One 2-inch piece of fresh ginger, peeled and thinly sliced
- 1 lemongrass stalk, tender inner bulb only, minced
- 2 fresh kaffir lime leaves
- 2 pounds butternut squash— peeled, seeded and cut into ½-inch dice (about 6 cups)
- ¼ cup Thai red curry paste
- 4 cups fish stock or bottled clam juice
- One 14-ounce can unsweetened coconut milk
- Kosher salt and freshly ground pepper

BOK CHOY
- 2 tablespoons vegetable oil
- 2 garlic cloves, minced
- 1 tablespoon minced peeled fresh ginger
- 2 pounds baby bok choy, leaves sliced lengthwise
- Kosher salt and freshly ground pepper

1 MAKE THE PICKLED MUSHROOMS In a medium saucepan, combine the sugar with both vinegars, the salt and ½ cup of water. Bring to a boil, stirring to dissolve the sugar. Remove from the heat and add the mushrooms, kaffir lime leaves and thyme and let stand until cooled completely. Transfer to a jar, cover and refrigerate until chilled, about 30 minutes.

2 MEANWHILE, MAKE THE SOUP In a large enameled cast-iron casserole, heat the oil until shimmering. Add the onion, garlic, ginger, lemongrass and kaffir lime leaves and cook over moderate heat, stirring occasionally, until softened and just starting to brown, about 8 minutes. Add the squash and red curry paste and cook, stirring, until the squash is coated and just starting to soften, about 10 minutes. Add the stock, coconut milk and 2 cups of water and bring to a boil. Simmer over moderately low heat, stirring occasionally, until the squash is very tender, about 25 minutes.

3 In batches, carefully puree the soup in a blender and transfer to a heatproof bowl. Strain the soup through a fine sieve back into the casserole and bring just to a simmer. Season with salt and pepper and keep warm.

4 PREPARE THE BOK CHOY In a large skillet, heat the oil until shimmering. Add the garlic and ginger and cook over moderately high heat, stirring, until fragrant, about 30 seconds. Add the bok choy and cook, tossing, until just wilted and crisp-tender, 2 to 3 minutes. Remove from the heat and season with salt and pepper.

5 Ladle the soup into shallow bowls, top with the bok choy and some of the pickled mushrooms and serve.

NOTE Kaffir lime leaves are the fragrant leaves of kaffir limes, a fruit native to Indonesia, Thailand and other parts of Southeast Asia. They are available at Southeast Asian and some Asian markets and online at *importfood.com.*

MAKE AHEAD The pickled mushrooms can be refrigerated in the pickling liquid for up to 1 week. The soup can be refrigerated for up to 3 days.

Habiger channels the flavors of Spain in two clever ways here:
He tosses grilled corn kernels in a smoked paprika aioli, then tops
the corn salad with red snapper fillets poached in chorizo-infused oil.

CHORIZO OIL–POACHED RED SNAPPER WITH GRILLED CORN SALAD

ACTIVE 45 min   **TOTAL** 2 hr   **MAKES** 4 servings

1 pound Spanish chorizo, cut into ½-inch pieces
3 cups canola oil, plus more for brushing
4 ears of corn, husked
Kosher salt and freshly ground pepper
½ cup mayonnaise
½ teaspoon finely grated lime zest
2 tablespoons fresh lime juice
1¼ teaspoons sweet smoked paprika
1 tablespoon extra-virgin olive oil
½ cup lightly packed cilantro, chopped
½ cup thinly sliced scallions
Four 6-ounce red snapper fillets with skin
Lime wedges, for serving

PAIR WITH Ripe, fruit-forward Chardonnay: 2011 Foxglove

1 In a food processor, pulse the chorizo until very finely chopped. Transfer to a deep 12-inch skillet, add the 3 cups of canola oil and cook over moderately low heat, stirring occasionally, until the oil is well flavored with the chorizo, about 1½ hours. Strain the chorizo oil through a fine sieve into a heatproof bowl; reserve the drained chorizo for another use (see Note). Return the strained oil to the skillet.

2 Meanwhile, light a grill or preheat a grill pan. Brush the corn with canola oil and season with salt and pepper. Grill over moderate heat, turning, until lightly charred and crisp-tender, 5 to 7 minutes. Transfer the corn to a plate and let cool completely, then cut the kernels off the cobs.

3 In a large bowl, whisk the mayonnaise with the lime zest and juice, smoked paprika and olive oil and season with salt and pepper. Fold in the corn kernels, cilantro and scallions.

4 Heat the chorizo oil until it reaches 160° on a candy thermometer; adjust the heat as necessary to maintain the temperature. Pat the fish fillets dry and season them with salt and pepper. Carefully slide the fillets into the chorizo oil and poach until just white throughout, about 12 minutes. If the fillets are not completely submerged in the oil, turn them halfway through poaching. Using a slotted spatula, transfer the fish to paper towels and blot dry. Serve with the grilled corn salad and lime wedges.

NOTE The drained chorizo can be spread on a foil-lined rimmed baking sheet and baked at 200° for about 2 hours, until crisp. The crispy chorizo bits can be sprinkled on salads, eggs or baked potatoes.

*Anderson and Habiger give this chicken layers of flavor by brining
it in a mix of sweet tea and thyme. After frying the chicken twice so it's
extra-crispy, they coat it in a sweet-and-spicy sauce of molasses,
cayenne pepper and gochujang (Korean chile paste).*

TEA-BRINED & DOUBLE-FRIED HOT CHICKEN

ACTIVE 1 hr   **TOTAL** 1 hr 30 min plus 24 hr brining   **MAKES** 4 servings

8 cups sweetened brewed tea
½ cup kosher salt, plus more
    for seasoning
10 thyme sprigs
1 head of garlic, halved crosswise,
    plus 3 garlic cloves
½ lemon, thinly sliced
4 chicken drumsticks
4 chicken thighs
3 tablespoons *gochujang*
    (see Note)
3 tablespoons sorghum molasses
1 tablespoon cayenne pepper
½ cup lard or 1 stick unsalted
    butter, softened
Canola oil, for frying
1½ cups all-purpose flour
½ cup Wondra flour
1½ tablespoons cornstarch
About 1 cup seltzer or club soda

PAIR WITH Ripe peach–scented
German Riesling with a touch
of sweetness: 2011 Gunderloch
Jean-Baptiste Kabinett

1 In a large saucepan, bring 4 cups of the sweet tea just to a boil. Add the ½ cup of kosher salt and stir until dissolved. Add the thyme, halved garlic head, lemon slices and the remaining 4 cups of sweet tea and let cool completely, then refrigerate until well chilled, about 45 minutes.

2 Add the chicken to the brine, cover and refrigerate for 24 to 48 hours.

3 Remove the chicken from the brine and pat dry with paper towels. Let stand at room temperature for 30 minutes.

4 Meanwhile, in a food processor, combine the 3 garlic cloves with the *gochujang*, molasses and cayenne and puree until a paste forms. Add the lard and puree until smooth. Season with salt. Scrape the mixture into a very large bowl.

5 In a large saucepan, heat 3 inches of oil until it reaches 350° on a candy thermometer. Set a rack over a rimmed baking sheet. Spread 1 cup of the all-purpose flour in a pie plate. In a medium bowl, whisk the remaining ½ cup of all-purpose flour with the Wondra flour, cornstarch and a generous pinch of salt. Whisk in ¾ cup of seltzer until a thick batter forms; add more seltzer if needed.

6 Dredge 4 of the chicken pieces in the flour, tap off the excess and transfer to the rack. Dip 1 piece of chicken at a time in the batter, let the excess drip back into the bowl and add the chicken to the hot oil. Fry the chicken at 350°, turning occasionally, until pale golden and crisp, about 8 minutes; return the chicken to the rack. Repeat with the remaining 4 pieces of chicken.

7 Return the first 4 pieces of chicken to the hot oil and fry at 350° until golden and an instant-read thermometer inserted in the thickest part registers 165°, 8 to 10 minutes. Drain on paper towels. Repeat with the remaining 4 pieces of chicken.

8 Add all of the fried chicken to the *gochujang* mixture and toss to coat. Transfer the chicken to a platter and serve right away.

NOTE *Gochujang,* Korean chile paste, is available at Asian markets.

RECIPE INDEX

CONTRIBUTORS

THE CHEFS

GRANT ACHATZ
Alinea, Next, The Aviary
all in Chicago alinearestaurant.com

ERIK ANDERSON
The Catbird Seat *Nashville*
thecatbirdseatrestaurant.com

JOHN BESH
August, Besh Steak, Domenica,
Soda Shop, The American Sector,
Borgne *all in New Orleans* Lüke
New Orleans; San Antonio La Provence
Lacombe, LA chefjohnbesh.com

STUART BRIOZA
State Bird Provisions *San Francisco*
statebirdsf.com

ANDREW CARMELLINI
Locanda Verde, Lafayette, The Public
Theater, Sausage Boss *all in New
York City* The Dutch *New York City;
Miami* andrewcarmellini.com

DAVID CHANG
Momofuku Noodle Bar *New York City;
Toronto* Momofuku Ko, Má Pêche,
Momofuku Ssäm Bar, Booker and Dax
all in New York City Momofuku Milk Bar
New York (seven locations); Toronto
Momofuku Nikai, Momofuku Daishō,
Momofuku Shōtō *all in Toronto*
Momofuku Seiōbo *Sydney* momofuku.com

ROY CHOI
Kogi BBQ trucks, Chego, Sunny Spot
all in Los Angeles area
A-Frame *Culver City, CA* kogibbq.com

TOM COLICCHIO
Craft *New York City; Los Angeles*
Craftsteak *Las Vegas; Foxwoods, CT*
'wichcraft *New York City; Las Vegas;
San Francisco* Craftbar, Colicchio &
Sons, Riverpark *all in New York City*
Topping Rose House *Bridgehampton, NY*
craftrestaurantsinc.com

MICHAEL CORDÚA
Churrascos *(three locations)*, Amazón Grill,
Américas Woodlands, Américas River Oaks,
Artista *all in Houston area* cordua.com

WYLIE DUFRESNE
WD-50, Alder *both in New York City*
wd-50.com

GRAHAM ELLIOT
Graham Elliot, G.E.B., Grahamwich
all in Chicago grahamelliot.com

JOSH HABIGER
Strategic Hospitality *Nashville*
strategichospitalityonline.com

LINTON HOPKINS
Restaurant Eugene, Holeman & Finch
Public House, H&F Bread Co., H&F Bottle
Shop *all in Atlanta* restauranteugene.com

DANIEL HUMM
Eleven Madison Park, The NoMad *both in
New York City* elevenmadisonpark.com

THOMAS KELLER
The French Laundry, Ad Hoc *both in
Yountville, CA* Per Se *New York City*
Bouchon Bistro *Yountville and
Beverly Hills, CA; Las Vegas* Bouchon
Bakery *Yountville and Beverly Hills,
CA; Las Vegas; New York City* tkrg.org

BARBARA LYNCH
No. 9 Park, Menton, Sportello, B&G Oysters,
The Butcher Shop, Drink, 9 at Home,
Stir *all in Boston* barbaralynch.com

NOBU MATSUHISA
Matsuhisa *Beverly Hills; Aspen and Vail,
CO; Athens and Mykonos, Greece*
Nobu *New York City; London; Milan;
Moscow; Tokyo; Cape Town; Perth,
Australia; and 16 other locations worldwide*
nobumatsuhisa.com

CARLO MIRARCHI
Roberta's, Blanca *both in
Brooklyn, NY* robertaspizza.com

NANCY OAKES
Boulevard, Prospect *both in San Francisco*
boulevard.com, prospectsf.com

DANIEL PATTERSON
Coi *San Francisco* Plum, Haven *both in
Oakland, CA* danielpattersongroup.com

ANNE QUATRANO
Bacchanalia, Abattoir, Quinones,
Floataway Cafe, Star Provisions
all in Atlanta starprovisions.com

ERIC RIPERT
Le Bernardin *New York City*
Blue by Eric Ripert *Grand Cayman,
Cayman Islands* aveceric.com

GABRIEL RUCKER
Le Pigeon, Little Bird
both in Portland, OR lepigeon.com

NANCY SILVERTON
Osteria Mozza *Los Angeles; Singapore*
Pizzeria Mozza *Los Angeles and Newport
Beach, CA; Singapore* osteriamozza.com

ETHAN STOWELL
Tavolàta, How to Cook a Wolf,
Anchovies & Olives, Staple & Fancy,
Rione XIII, Bar Cotto *all in Seattle*
ethanstowellrestaurants.com

MICHAEL SYMON
Lola, Lolita *both in Cleveland*
Roast *Detroit* B Spot *Cleveland (three
locations), Westlake, Woodmere
and Strongsville, OH* lolabistro.com

FOOD PHOTOGRAPHER

CHRIS COURT *all food images*

FOOD STYLIST

JUSTINE POOLE *all food images*

CHEF PORTRAIT PHOTOGRAPHERS

CEDRIC ANGELES
*Michael Cordúa, page 70; Erik Anderson
and Josh Habiger, page 250*

JAKE CHESSUM
*Tom Colicchio, page 40;
Eric Ripert, page 50*

PAUL COSTELLO
*Anne Quatrano, page 80;
John Besh, page 120;
Linton Hopkins, page 220*

BOBBY FISHER
*Gabriel Rucker, page 200; Ethan Stowell,
page 210; Roy Choi, page 230*

ETHAN HILL
*Nobu Matsuhisa, page 20;
Barbara Lynch, page 90; Michael Symon,
page 110; Wylie Dufresne, page 140;
Grant Achatz, page 150*

MARCUS NILSSON
David Chang, page 190

PEDEN + MUNK
*Thomas Keller, page 10; Nancy Silverton,
page 30; Nancy Oakes, page 60;
Daniel Patterson, page 100; Stuart Brioza,
page 160; Graham Elliot, page 170*

MICHAEL TUREK
*Andrew Carmellini, page 130;
Carlo Mirarchi, page 240*

BJÖRN WALLANDER
Daniel Humm, page 180

FOOD&WINE
BOOKS

More books from

FOOD&WINE

ANNUAL COOKBOOK
An entire year of FOOD & WINE recipes from cooks
around the world: more than 600 simple and
fabulous dishes, all perfected in our Test Kitchen.

BEST OF THE BEST
In one definitive volume, over 100 tantalizing recipes from
the best cookbooks of the year, chosen by FOOD & WINE.

COCKTAILS
Over 120 incredible cocktail recipes and dozens of fantastic
dishes from America's most acclaimed mixologists
and chefs, plus an indispensable guide to cocktail basics.

WINE GUIDE
An essential, pocket-size guide focusing on the world's most
reliable producers, with an easy-to-use food pairing primer.

To order, call 800-284-4145
or log on to **foodandwine.com/books**